The Kindertransport

The Kindertransport

What Really Happened

ANDREA HAMMEL

polity

First published in 2024 by Polity Press

Polity Press
65 Bridge Street
Cambridge CB2 1UR, UK

Polity Press
111 River Street
Hoboken, NJ 07030, USA

ISBN-13: 978-1-5095-5376-1
ISBN-13: 978-1-5095-5377-8 (pb)

A catalogue record for this book is available from the British Library.

Library of Congress Control Number: 2023934601

Typeset in 11 on 14pt Warnock Pro
by Cheshire Typesetting Ltd, Cuddington, Cheshire
Printed and bound in Great Britain by CPI Group (UK) Ltd, Croydon

For further information on Polity, visit our website:
politybooks.com

Contents

Acknowledgements

This book is the culmination of nearly 25 years of research, conferences, communication, writing, re-writing, networking and interviewing. I am especially grateful to Stephanie van Limpt-Homer, Nick Hubble, Julia Davies and all at Polity Press for their faith in my ideas and my writing.

I am grateful to all the Kindertransport refugees who were willing to talk to me. I learnt so much.

I would also like to thank the following:

Tasha Alden, Sylvia Asmus, Ruth Barnett, Wolfgang Benz, Martha Blend, Monica Bohm-Duchen, Charmian Brinson, Morris Brodie, Renate Collins, Michael Couchman, Claudia Curio, Winifred V. Davies, Ellen Davis, Sylvia Degen, Rachel Dieneman, William Dieneman, Lucy Duncanson, Clive Evans, Tony Friedlander, Christoph Gann, Gábor Gelléri, Anthony Grenville, Anita H. Grosz, Melissa Hacker, Gale Halpern, Alex Hammel, Max Hammel, Sara Hammel, Andrew Hesketh, Joanne Hopkins, Gaby Koppel, Tony Kushner, Bea Lewkowicz, Ingrid Lumfors, Alex Maws, Tamara Meyer, Bill Niven, Gloria Ogborn, Christoph Ribbat, Angelika Rieber, Matthias Schirmer, Barbara Schreiber, Ruth Schwiening, Anne Senchal, Rose Simpson, Elena Spagnuolo, Monja Stahlberger,

Karen Stuke, Janet Thomas, Moira Vincentelli, Godela Weiss-Sussex, Heidi Wiener, Norbert Wiesneth and Amy Williams; the members and trustees of Aberaid; my students and colleagues at Aberystwyth University, and especially at the Centre for the Movement of People (CMOP) and the Modern Languages Department; the members of the Research Centre for German and Austrian Exile Studies and the Gesellschaft für Exilforschung e.V.; the members and elders of St David's Church in Aberystwyth.

Abbreviations

AJEX	Association of Jewish Ex-Servicemen
AJR	Association of Jewish Refugees
BCRC	British Committee for Refugees from Czechoslovakia
CBF/WJR	Central British Fund for German Jewry / World Jewish Relief
IKG	Israelitische Kultusgemeinde Wien (Jewish Community in Vienna)
KTA	Kindertransport Association (North America)
PJRF	Polish Jewish Refugee Fund
RCM	Refugee Children's Movement

1

Myth

There is history and there is myth, and they are not the same thing. In the category of myth come those tales nations tell themselves to feel virtuous, even heroic.[1]

In the night between 9 and 10 May 1939, at 2.50 a.m., 12-year-old Eva Mosbacher said goodbye to her parents Hedwig and Otto Mosbacher and joined a group of three boys and two other girls on a train at Nuremberg Station. In Munich, she joined another train, and they all changed again at Frankfurt for a long journey to London. While still travelling, Eva started writing a long letter to her parents left behind at home. She asked them whether they managed to get back to sleep after seeing her off and described the dialect of the children who had joined her on the way. Eva seems a very astute girl, showing unusual reflection and empathy towards her parents, almost indicating a role reversal in her letter. She writes: 'The worst must be over for you now, you were very brave. I did not manage quite without tears.' And goes on to describe that she saw some more goodbyes between children and their parents 'that were dreadful'.[2]

Eva Mosbacher was fleeing National Socialist persecution in Germany on a Kindertransport. The term 'Kindertransport' describes both the individual transports and the overarching scheme that allowed over 10,000 unaccompanied minors, mainly with Jewish backgrounds, from Germany, Austria, Czechoslovakia and Poland, to escape Nazism and find refuge in the UK between December 1938 and September 1939.

The Mosbachers were a Jewish family, and their life had changed dramatically after Adolf Hitler became German chancellor on 30 January 1933 and the subsequent rapid National Socialist takeover of Germany. The well-established family had been ostracized, and both Hedwig's family and Otto had to close their respective family firms because of discriminations and policies that robbed Jewish businesses of their opportunities and their assets. From 1937 onwards, Eva's parents tried to find a way to leave Germany and find sanctuary elsewhere. Hedwig and Otto Mosbacher applied for a visa to the USA, which had a quota system for immigrants from different countries. This meant that Jewish refugees from Germany were given a number on a list. The couple also looked into the possibility of fleeing to Cuba or South Africa. In 1938, they thought that it might take at least another two years before they would be granted a visa to the USA. Like most in Germany on 9 and 10 November 1938, the family were shocked by the widespread violence of the November Pogrom against Jewish people and Jewish property. Sometimes called 'Kristallnacht' on account of the large amount of broken glass that it left in the street, this state-sponsored violence included the destruction of synagogues and other Jewish institutions and businesses, numerous arson attacks, and the incarceration, beating and even murder of Jews, mainly men. This happened in Vienna and Berlin and other German towns and cities such as Nuremberg, where the Mosbachers lived, and also in villages and rural communities.

In Nuremburg alone, nine Jews were murdered by Nazi thugs, and the Orthodox synagogue, which had been used by the other Jewish congregations as well, was attacked by arsonists and burnt down. All over the German Reich, Jewish men were arrested and incarcerated in concentration camps. Otto Mosbacher's older brother Kurt, a lawyer in Munich, was arrested and taken to Dachau concentration camp where he was imprisoned for four weeks. For many Jewish families, the experience of the November Pogrom acted as the last straw. They were now willing to consider any measure that might enable family members to leave Germany, even under previously unthinkable conditions, such as separating children from parents. Eva's parents decided to send her to the UK on a Kindertransport in the hope that eventually the whole family would be able to make it to the USA together, and that Eva would stay in the safety of the UK in the meantime. The Mosbachers had more connections to the UK than most: Eva's cousin had lived in Cambridge since 1936 and was in a position to contact the Cambridge Refugee Committee to help her find foster parents.

Eva reports that the youngest refugee on the train was a 6-month-old baby and wrote to her parents: 'You can count yourselves lucky that I am already 12.' Her foster placement was with two Christian women in Cambridge, women with professional careers in healthcare and academia, and the means and the desire to help a young refugee. They lived in a large house just outside Cambridge and were warm, insightful and caring. Soon after her arrival, on 15 May 1939, Eva started attending the Perse School for Girls in Cambridge and got moved up a year immediately. Over the next years, Eva kept up an intense correspondence with her parents and continued to hope that Hedwig and Otto would join her soon, writing in one letter 'when we are together again, we will have achieved a lot'. In other letters, Eva described a happy and educationally quite successful life of a teenage girl, while her parents' emigration attempts were always foremost in her mind: 'Hopefully your Cuba plans will work out. School holidays. Report good, I am

busy. Got invited to the theatre by my best friend. You are
always in my thoughts, and I wish you all the best.'

Her parents back home suffered under the intensified persecution from the Nazis and continued to try to get out of
Germany. In the following years, they bought ship's passages
twice: from Kobe to the USA, due to depart on 17 November
1940, and from Lisbon to New York, due to depart on
10 October 1941, but in neither case did they manage to get
the necessary visa for entry to the USA. After Eva had left,
the Mosbacher parents had moved to Hedwig's home town of
Meiningen in Thuringia, and in October 1941 they were forced
to move to the ghetto house, or 'Jew house', in Meiningen.
They wrote to their daughter: 'We have to put up with a lot
that cannot be changed, but we still hope that we will get
an opportunity to travel before it is finally too late.' Three
years to the day after their daughter fled on a Kindertransport
to the UK, however, they were deported from Thuringia to
Belzyce together with 1,000 other German Jews of all ages.
There, Eva's parents were murdered. Their last message
to Eva was dated 3 May 1942, and they said that they were
'trying to be brave' and that they 'were with her in their
thoughts'.[3]

Eva did not find out about the death of her parents until
years later. The sudden cessation of correspondence affected
her badly. But, of course, she had no choice but to carry on
with her life in the UK. Despite the tragic loss of her parents,
in the 1940s and 1950s, Eva seemed to be doing well: she got on
with her foster mothers, she stayed at the Perse School for Girls
until 1944, and planned to train as a nurse. She delayed the
start of her training, taking care of one of her foster mothers,
who had become ill. Eventually, Eva trained at Addenbrooke's
Hospital in Cambridge and at North Cambridgeshire Hospital
in Wisbech, successfully completing her training in 1950. Her
final report describes her as very caring towards her patients
but sometimes lacking in self-confidence. In the post-war

Eva Mosbacher   Hedwig Mosbacher   Otto Mosbacher
With permission from Christoph Gann

years, Eva worked as a registered nurse, moved to London, and eventually lived in Wimbledon, renting a room in the house of a German Jewish lawyer.

On 10 November 1963, Eva Mosbacher took her own life in a hotel near Victoria Station in London.

The Kindertransport is often discussed and remembered as a generous, humanitarian rescue scheme, and the emphasis of public discussion is on escape, survival and a successful life in the UK. It is cited by the media as a heroic scheme and used as evidence for a history of generous humanity towards refugees. In March 2022, for example, after Russia invaded Ukraine and many Ukrainians, especially women and children, were looking for refuge in European countries, including the UK, the commentator Simon Heffer said on the BBC Radio 4's *Broadcasting House* programme: 'We have a noble tradition of looking after refugees: I think back to the Kindertransport.' But is this true?

Eva Mosbacher had to leave her parents behind in Germany, as the UK did not allow them to seek sanctuary with her, and their desperate attempts to escape came to nothing. Eva had to live with the fact that, while she was saved, they were not and were murdered in the Holocaust. Eva clearly could not

cope with this; she took her own life on the anniversary of the
November Pogrom – the day when it became clear to many
Jews of the German Reich that they had to escape urgently.
Eva's parents did not manage to escape. Had the family
been able to flee to the UK together, things might have been
different.

Like Eva, the large majority of child refugees who fled on
a Kindertransport were not orphans. They had parents and
families. In most cases, the families initially tried to escape
National Socialist persecution as a family unit, or at least in a
way that one parent could accompany the child. But the UK
government (and most governments around the world) made
it very difficult for refugees to find sanctuary in their respective
countries. In the case of the Kindertransport, the UK stipulated that only those under 18 years of age could be admitted.
This fact is often forgotten.

Examining the history of the first half of the century shows
that the UK became increasingly restrictive to sanctuary seekers. Until early in the twentieth century, entry into the UK by
foreign nationals was largely unregulated. The Aliens Act of
1905 sought to regulate immigration and demanded that those
coming to the UK should be in possession of sufficient means
to support themselves. However, it privileged those claiming
to flee persecution for religious or political reasons, and stated
that such persons should not automatically be refused entry
even if they could not prove that they could support themselves. This was the so-called 'asylum clause'. Internationally,
this was the first law to define refugee status. The Aliens Act
1905 was introduced in large parts in response to an increase
in Russian and Eastern European Jews wishing to come and
settle in the UK to escape anti-Semitic pogroms and persecution after 1880. Anti-foreign sentiments, fears about too many
poor immigrants, and anti-Semitism all played a part in the
introduction of this law. The hostilities of the First World War
moved the UK Parliament to introduce the Aliens Restriction

Act 1914 in response to security fears regarding German and Austrian immigrants. This meant that refugees fleeing National Socialism, the majority of whom were Jewish and German or at least German-speaking, were met with ingrained antipathy from some members of the public, sections of the media, parts of the government, and other political groups. Subsequently, the 1919 Aliens Restriction Act removed the 'asylum clause' of the 1905 Act, and therefore refugees could not claim special status and were treated like other immigrants and subject to general immigration policy.

It is a fact that in the 1930s the UK government's policy was not laying the foundation for a noble tradition: it was mainly concerned with keeping refugees fleeing Nazism away from the UK, rather than aiding their escape. There were, of course, exceptions among Parliamentarians, such as Eleanor Rathbone MP and Josiah Wedgwood MP, who both campaigned tirelessly on behalf of refugees. There was also the Anglo-Jewish community who tried to assist Continental Jewish refugees and lobbied on their behalf, and initially assured the government that they would cover the cost of those arriving without any means of support. Last, but by no means least, there were thousands of ordinary citizens who viewed the persecution on the Continent with great concern and wanted to assist its desperate victims in any way they could. They organized and raised money, they fostered child refugees and assisted in different ways.

Rather than a UK government-led scheme, the Kindertransport was a hastily assembled visa waiver scheme, restricted to those under the age of 18. It was introduced following the November Pogrom on 9 and 10 November 1938, which was widely reported on in the British media. Ordinary citizens put pressure on the government and urged it to come to the aid of the persecuted Jews of the German Reich. But rather than relaxing the visa rules, the government would only agree to an exception for minors.

One reason why the Kindertransport scheme was restricted to minors was over fears that adult refugees might compete with British people on the labour market for jobs in this period of high unemployment. Children were not likely to seek jobs soon after their arrival. Children who were accommodated in foster families were also not likely to pose a financial burden to the UK state. The Kindertransport scheme was not funded by the government but financed by charities and donations. In fact, the government demanded that a guarantee of £50 be lodged for every child refugee admitted to the UK to indemnify the UK government against any future expense: child refugees 'should not become a burden on the public purse'. This was a large sum of money at the time, roughly equivalent to £3,500 today. The requirement to raise this guarantee was the main reason why it was not possible to get more children to the UK at the time.

More than 10,000 child refugees were part of a Kindertransport between December 1938 and September 1939, a short period of ten months. On the one hand, this is a remarkable achievement. On the other hand, the lack of government support in funding and organizational terms also resulted in issues that led to serious problems for some Kindertransport refugees once they had arrived in the UK. There was little support for the child refugees themselves to cope with the experience of being persecuted, uprooted, and separated from their parents. Even those who arrived with siblings were often separated from them. There was little attempt to match the child refugees and the foster placements using clear criteria. There was insufficient effort made to match religious and cultural backgrounds of children and foster placements. Most of the children chosen were Jewish, but the vast majority of potential foster families were not (as the Jewish population in the UK was small). There also was a lack of vetting of the placements with disastrous consequences for some. Many had to change placements several times: some children were neglected, some were exploited, and some were physically or sexually abused. Some foster parents thought that they would be able to adopt the child refugee and did not acknowledge that the children had birth parents who just wanted them to be looked after for a period of time and had not agreed to such a move.

There was also little initial support for the foster parents and others in charge of caring for the Kindertransport refugees, and very little preparation for the complicated task all of them faced. Nor was there sufficient ongoing support. Many had envisaged that the children's placements would be needed for a matter of months; however, in most cases, they were needed for years.

Additionally, because there was no overall policy that governed the selection of children for a Kindertransport, and no rules regarding priorities and who was to be considered a suitable candidate or an urgent case, the scheme can be criticized for not sufficiently recognizing potential bias. The Kindertransport in general excluded children with additional needs, such as children with physical disabilities, learning difficulties, chronic illnesses (such as diabetes) and mental health problems. Even children with minor behavioural problems such as bed-wetting were often excluded. All the Continental organizations in the different countries had to make tough decisions, but it was the Refugee Children's Movement, the umbrella organizing body in the UK, that had the final decision-making power.

This book will provide a critical history of the Kindertransport, drawing on a broad range of sources. It will outline how the policy framework for the Kindertransport was established, by looking at parliamentary records; it will look at the organization of the Kindertransport both on the Continent and in the UK by using the organizational archival material available and letters and other material from organizers. The book will also look at how the Kindertransport was experienced by individual child refugees, their birth parents and their foster parents and others involved in their placement in the UK, as revealed in archival material and personal recollections. Last, but not least, we will try to reflect the emotions and opinions of the Kindertransport refugees themselves, looking at their testimony. Many of them gave interviews and many wrote memoirs – some were published and some were given to archives or kept privately. Over the last forty years, different narratives of Kindertransport history have emerged. After the Kindertransport refugees got together in several organized reunions in the late 1980s and early 1990s, some very positive celebratory narratives of the Kindertransport were published or told. Many former child refugees felt that they wanted to express their gratitude for being saved in their recollections. It can be argued that this led to an exclusion of more critical narratives as, initially, few stories talked about the painful parts of their experiences. Nevertheless, all these voices have to be credited for bringing the Kindertransport scheme to the attention of researchers and the public.

Later academic accounts of Kindertransport history have been much more critical of the scheme. The earliest book-length publication in English was very uncritical of the organization of the Kindertransport: Barry Turner's ... *And the Policeman Smiled: 10,000 Children Escape from Nazi Europe* presents a very positive view of the Kindertransport experience and thus of the UK's decision to admit only unaccompanied child refugees.[4] Turner was commissioned to write this book by World Jewish Relief, the successor organization to the Refugee Children's Movement that assisted the Kindertransport refugees in the 1930s and 1940s. He was able to use the archives of the World Jewish Relief Fund, which contain many case files of Kindertransportees. These files have since been closed to researchers and are only accessible to the former refugees and their descendants. Turner's book allows no verification as he fails to include either references to the material used or any explanation as to the method of selection.

More critical books followed after the increase in public attention and the rise in the number of published memoirs from the early 1990s onwards. The first book-length research monograph was written by Rebekka Göpfert in German and published in Germany in 1999.[5] The study uses 27 oral history interviews conducted by the author, and archival material available at the time. It maps out the field but is by necessity focused on the experience of a relatively small number of people. One of the most interesting aspects of this study is the different experiences it reveals for former Kindertransport refugees who eventually settled in the USA, in comparison to those who settled in the UK. Those living in the USA felt much more integrated in their community and country – which, after all, champions the immigration experience – than those who had lived in the UK since the Second World War, who continued to feel that they were outsiders and defined by their refugee experience. The first study of the Kindertransport from an organizational angle was published by Claudia Curio in 2006, also in German, which might have resulted in its findings not being analysed and built upon in further studies as they should have been.[6]

Over many years, the historian Tony Kushner consistently presented a very critical analysis of the government policy that led to the organization of the Kindertransport, and of the use of Kindertransport memorialization in public and political discourse in the UK. He published a number of articles and chapters in his works on refugees. Additionally, he supervised two doctoral theses which were eventually published as critical monographs: Louise London published the very detailed *Whitehall and the Jews 1933–1948: British Immigration Policy and the Holocaust* in 2000.[7] London fits the Kindertransport scheme into her much larger remit of an investigation of British immigration policy and shows how the scheme fits in with ideological changes and newly developed regulations. She is highly critical of both the Kindertransport scheme and the wider policies of the time, as well as of the sectarian nature of the British Jewish community. Jennifer Craig-Norton's 2019 monograph *The Kindertransport: Contesting Memory* derives from the same school of thought.[8] It is very detailed, and especially comprehensive regarding lesser-known experiences such as the history of the Kindertransport refugees who escaped from the Polish border region to the UK. Her focus on this very specific – and smallest – group of Kindertransport refugees occasionally leads her to draw conclusions from a minority experience and generalize for Kindertransport refugees as a whole.

Both Vera K. Fast's *Children's Exodus* and Judith Tydor Baumel-Schwartz's *Never Look Back* are especially informative regarding the experience of Orthodox Jewish children.[9] The minority of Kindertransport refugees were from Orthodox families, and most placements in the UK were not run according to Orthodox traditions. The two books provide opposing interpretations of the appropriateness of the provision for such children, both during the organization of transports and after their arrival.

However, none of these books has managed to reach beyond the circle of experts in the field. Many interested members of the public still do not have an adequate grasp of the history of the Kindertransport. They do not have detailed knowledge of the extent to which it was a government scheme, how it relied on volunteers and charitable organizations, what happened to the birth parents of the child refugees and the challenges the refugees faced in the UK. This is why the Kindertransport is still sometimes referred to as a UK government humanitarian success, as part of a noble tradition. This book is trying to fill this gap in public awareness.

The 80th commemoration of the Kindertransport in 2018–19 resulted in increased attention for the historic events. It is likely that this will be matched in 2023–4 during the Kindertransport's 85th commemoration, which will be the last time when we can realistically expect any involvement in events and public discussions from former Kindertransport refugees themselves.

Comparisons are often drawn between the Kindertransport and the UK's handling of those seeking sanctuary in the UK today. This is understandable, but, if we want to compare, we need to understand Kindertransport history fully. This book combines research with readability, providing a critical analysis of archival sources and, at the same time, bringing a wide range of voices – voices of eyewitnesses and survivors – to the fore. Most readers are fascinated by the life histories of Kindertransport refugees and want to learn more about their experience and how it affected them.

But we also need to look at other sources that show us how the government and the organizations of the time acted. Thus, the self-reflexive narratives will be complemented by the results of my archival research conducted over more than twenty years. I have looked at organizational documents in both English and German, located in Austria, Germany, Israel and the UK. I am convinced that only by combined analysis of these different sources can we do justice to the complex phenomenon of the Kindertransport. I will start by discussing the context of the child refugees' flight. I will examine the persecution and violence they experienced in Germany, Austria, Czechoslovakia and Poland. I will look at the organization of the Kindertransport on both sides of the Channel, and the experience of the children who were selected – in contrast to those who were rejected – for a place on a Kindertransport to the UK, as well as what happened to their parents and families who could not flee with them. A central part of this book will document the very varied and difficult times the children had at their initial and subsequent placements in foster families, boarding schools, training camps and children's homes. We also have to remember that many Kindertransport refugees and their descendants are our fellow citizens, in the UK but also in the USA (as many migrated farther). When the Kindertransport was first organized in 1938, almost everyone involved in the organization and the support of the scheme vastly underestimated the time the children would spend in their placements and in the UK. The children inevitably grew older and changed between 1938–9 and 1945, and the events of the Second World War also left their mark on everyone involved. The end of the war provided them with new opportunities and with new challenges. We do not have any reliable data to be able to say with certainty how many of those fleeing via the Kindertransport scheme saw their parents again after the war, and how many lost one or both of their parents. The experience of being separated, losing contact during the war, and finding out their parents' fate, needs to be discussed in detail. Even those who were reunited with their parents, or other members of their family, had to cope with the rupture the events of the war and the Holocaust had caused. Most such reunions were far from easy, happy occasions.

A substantial number of Kindertransport refugees left the UK and migrated farther to other countries. The history of the Kindertransport is therefore not just part of British history, as it is sometimes believed, but part of other national histories as well, although I have to leave a more detailed discussion of those experiences to other colleagues and books. A very small number returned to live in the countries of their birth.

Some Kindertransport refugees have led very prominent lives, such as the Labour Peer Lord Alf Dubs, the artist Frank Auerbach, the entrepreneur Dame Steve Shirley or the Nobel Prize-winners Walter Kohn and Leslie Baruch Brent. As can be expected, most led more ordinary lives, though often succeeding professionally or in their private endeavours. However, there were also those who suffered from physical and mental ill health due to the trauma of their early years, and then there were those like Eva Mosbacher who decided that they could not continue and ended their lives. The positive stories have to be balanced with the tragic ones to show the real long-term consequences of the Kindertransport scheme.

2

Persecution

The Nazis in Germany had already perpetrated discrimination and violent acts against Jews on a semi-illegal level before they came into power in early 1933. Jewish citizens had been attacked in the street by the paramilitary arms of the Nazi Party and other affiliated right-wing groups. Anti-Semitism manifested itself in verbal attacks and discriminatory practices – especially regarding employment, but really in all areas of life. Like many countries in Europe, Germany had a long history of anti-Semitism. However, what would follow the National Socialist Party's ascent to power after 30 January 1933 was of a vastly different order.

There were around 525,000 Jewish men, women and children in Germany in 1933, which was only about 0.75 per cent of the overall population.[1] Nevertheless, Nazi propaganda painted them as a threat to the 'Aryan' population of Germany. After the Nazi takeover in January 1933, persecution of Jews became active Nazi policy. This was at first hindered by the lack of agreement on the definition of who was considered Jewish and who was considered Aryan. Nazi ideologues agreed that racial definitions should be based first and foremost on biological heritage, i.e. bloodlines, not present-day religious affiliations or self-definition, but they initially could not agree 'how much' Jewish blood would mark an individual out as Jewish. A complicated system regarding those of mixed heritage was constructed, which defined anyone with at least one Jewish grandparent as Jewish. For some individuals, and especially for some children, this meant that they only became aware of their Jewish heritage through the implementation of this Nazi definition and the resulting discrimination and persecution.

On 1 April 1933, the Nazis instigated a public boycott of Jewish businesses and shops throughout Germany. Six days later, the Law for the Restoration of the Professional Civil Service was passed, banning Jews from civil service and government jobs. On an ideological level, this was deemed necessary to prevent the infiltration of damaging 'non-Aryan' hereditary traits into the German racial community. On a more practical level, it was argued that the Jews had been trying to take over certain areas of the professions and the civil service. For many middle-class Jewish families, this meant a sudden change in income and status. This change is something a few of the older Kindertransport refugees would later remember. From 1933 onwards, many Jewish businesses were also 'aryanized', which, even in this early phase, often meant they were taken away from their Jewish owners without compensation. Kindertransport refugee Marion Charles remembered how her father lost his manufacturing business and recorded at the time that he 'now helps mother with household chores and even peels potatoes'.[2]

Although it is difficult to analyse conclusively what effect the National Socialist anti-Semitic policies had on children, as compared to adults, the growing exclusion of Jewish children from mainstream schools in Germany had a direct effect on them. The implementation of the law euphemistically called the Law against the Overcrowdedness of German Schools and Universities, which in reality was aimed at excluding Jews, was an important change for most children and young people defined as Jewish. This law was passed in April 1933. Again, the

Nazi rationale had been that Jewish children and young people were taking over the more prestigious German educational institutions. A quota for the admission of Jewish children to German schools was set, and many Jewish children were explicitly asked to leave their schools. Others report that they were asked to sit in a different place from before, separately or at the back, or that they were ignored by their fellow pupils and their teachers. Often their parents decided to move them to Jewish schools, which some experienced as a relief and some as a great loss of their old school environment. Even for those who were still enrolled in mainstream German schools, every-day life was increasingly affected: they were excluded from school trips and other extra-curricular activities; they were banned from swimming pools and cinemas. Many felt more and more ostracized. Many experienced discrimination and persecution in public life – for example, on their journeys to and from school. Kindertransport refugee Edith Milton wrote about her desire to hide on her way to school: 'I shrink against the privet hedge, trying to be invisible, and am preparing myself to run away.'[3] Ruth Oppenheimer (later Ruth David) recalls that she decided that 'she no longer wanted to be out of doors, life seemed too unsafe'.[4] These changes in attitude and treatment from friends and acquaintances must have been dif-ficult to comprehend for many, especially for younger children who had less understanding of the political context, and even more so for those who had not been aware of their Jewish background before the Nazi rise to power.

Kindertransport refugee Beate Maria Siegel (later Bea Green) remembers anti-Semitism at school, and her father being beaten by the Nazis. Bea was born in 1925 into a Jewish family in the Bogenhausen district of Munich. Her family was educated and wealthy and led a comfortable life in the Bavarian capital. Bea had started attending primary school from 1931 and, as early as her second year there in 1932, she remembers her teacher making anti-Semitic remarks. She recalls that the teacher was meant to provide the children with pencils and other necessary material for their schoolwork, but when Bea asked for a new pencil, the teacher said: 'Don't you Jew children have enough money to buy your own?' Bea remembered that her mother was very annoyed when she told her parents about this remark, which she initially found puzzling.

Bea's father, Dr Michael Siegel, was a lawyer with his own legal practice in Munich. Like many other Jewish professionals, especially those in the legal profession, he felt that even though Germany had a new government, the rule of law and the principles of justice were still valid. On 10 March 1933, he went to the Police Headquarters in Munich to file a complaint on behalf of a client, a Mr Uhlfelder who owned a well-known Munich department store, regarding Uhlfelder's unwarranted arrest. When Siegel arrived at the police station, he was put in a room with Nazi storm troopers (SA), many of whom had been given jobs as auxiliary policemen in February 1933. These men violently assaulted Dr Siegel, knocking out teeth and perforating one of his ear drums, as well as cutting off his trouser legs, probably in order to make him look ridiculous and less professional. He was then marched through the Munich streets with a hand-painted sign around his neck reading 'I will never again complain to the police.' The thugs even threatened to kill him. Fortunately, he managed to escape when he reached the area around the main station in Munich by jumping into a taxi and getting the driver to take him home to relative safety.

Bea was 8 years old when this happened, and she vividly remembered the incident in later life. She was off school with a cold, and alone upstairs in their large flat as her mother had gone shopping and the maid was doing laundry downstairs. When she heard someone in the corridor near her room, she was surprised that the returning party did not look in on her and left her bed to investigate. She found her father's suit drenched in blood hanging in the corridor, which shocked her:

Dr Michael Siegel
Sueddeutsche Zeitung Photo / Alamy Stock Photo

So . . . I tiptoed down the corridor, the length of the corridor, to
my parents' bedroom which was opposite the main door, and
I did something I had never done in my life, I knocked on my
parents' bedroom door, no answer, so I opened it gingerly and
just saw my father pull up the bedclothes, so I shouldn't see his
face, only his eyes were showing, and he mumbled: 'Wait until
your mother gets home.' . . . So I crept out again and went back
to bed. And I remember lying on my back, feeling not very
good, feeling kind of empty. I suppose I was really scared.. . .
My mum came home, and the maid came home. And there was
a lot of talk, but never in front of me.[5]

The family retreated to their holiday home in the Bavarian
village of Walchensee and the father recovered. This incident
shows the complex situation of a professional Jewish family at

the time. The father still felt it was right and proper to complain to the police about an unwarranted arrest of a Jewish citizen, they could still retreat to their holiday home (it was later expropriated) and they tried to protect their young daughter from the harsh reality of anti-Semitic persecution at the time. But they had lost the comfort and security of their former lives.

By chance, the public spectacle of Michael Siegel being marched through the street was captured by the photographer Heinrich Sanden. Unsurprisingly, the German press were not interested in publishing the photographs, but Sanden offered them to an American photographer at International News Reel and the story and the photograph were widely published in the US press, including the *Washington Times*, as an illustration of abuse and brutality in Nazi Germany.[6]

Despite this violent attack on Bea's father in the early months of the Nazi regime, the Siegel family was reluctant to leave Germany. Michael Siegel initially felt defiant and wanted to stay there as he did not think the Nazis should have the power to make him leave his fatherland. The family felt strongly Bavarian and German. Later, he felt that he could not consider giving up his career. As a German lawyer, he was only able to practise in Germany. However, due to the increasing persecution and exclusion, by 1937 the Siegel parents changed their mind and decided that they wanted to leave the country. But by then they could not find anywhere to go and had also lost some of their wealth. They considered Palestine and the UK, but could not get an entry visa for either. Michael did not feel he was able to apply to work as a butler, despite the fact that getting a job in domestic service was one of the few ways to get a visa for the UK. The parents did, however, decide to send their son and daughter to the UK. Bea arrived on a Kindertransport in England aged 14, and was fostered by a wealthy older woman who was very supportive and enabled her to have a private education and, eventually, to go to university. The Siegel parents continued to live in Munich until 1940, when they were lucky enough to be able to escape to Peru at this late stage. They travelled east via the trans-Siberian railroad from Berlin across the Soviet Union and by ship to Japan, and then across the Pacific to Lima. After the Second World War, the mother visited her children in the UK, and eventually the whole family was able to meet up again in South America. Dr Siegel died in Lima in 1979 at the age of 96. Bea lived for two years in Peru, but made her long-term home in London, speaking about her experiences frequently and donating some of her possessions from her earlier life to the Imperial War Museum in London. Bea attended the opening of the new Second World War and Holocaust Galleries there in October 2021.

From the viewpoint of the twenty-first century, with our knowledge of the history of the Holocaust, the reluctance of German Jewish families to leave the German Reich quickly after the Nazi takeover seems astonishing. But it is unhelpful to judge people for being reluctant to leave their homes and lives. It was mainly the politically active, especially communists and socialists, who escaped during the early years of the Nazi regime, as it was abundantly clear to them that there would be no place for political opponents in Nazi Germany. However, many Jews without those affiliations hesitated to make concrete preparations for emigration, even though Jewish organizations began discussing this option soon after the Nazi rise to power. The German Jewish Board of Deputies decided very quickly that leaving Germany was the only way to save the lives and livelihoods of many German Jews, and thus decided to promote and facilitate emigration. This soon became one of the main tasks of the organization; they had an Emigration Department and a separate Department for Child Emigration. The emigration of minors without their parents or families was also discussed early on, but initially it seems that organizations within the Jewish community were not keen to advocate such a solution. In an article in the newsletter of the Association of Jewish Women in Germany, the author states categorically in 1933: 'We should refrain from advocating the emigration of unaccompanied minors.'[7] But clearly the intensification of the persecution suffered by Jews between 1933 and 1938 changed this.

It is shocking how many Jewish children experienced an abrupt change regarding their treatment by their non-Jewish friends. Some remember this change in their relationship as happening overnight. They recall being swiftly excluded from friendship groups and ignored after the Nazi takeover, an extremely painful experience for any child. This happened to Ruth David and her older sister Hannah, who had been friends with a boy next door who stopped playing with them suddenly.[8]

Despite the fact that some changes felt very sudden to Jewish children, the exclusion of Jews from civil society in Germany happened over a number of years. The Nuremberg Race Laws that came into effect in 1935 regulated matters relating to relationships, including sexual relationships and marriages between Jews and non-Jews and matters of so-called 'racial purity'. Many Kindertransport refugees later related how these laws affected their families, especially if one of their parents was Jewish and the other was not. It also stopped non-Jews from being employed in Jewish households, and vice versa. Many middle-class Jewish children remembered that they had to part with beloved nannies and housekeepers. For working-class Jewish families, it meant a further restriction regarding employment opportunities as they could not now work for non-Jewish employers.

For Jewish families in Austria, its annexation by Nazi Germany on 12 March 1938 brought a much quicker change than in Germany. All anti-Semitic legislation was brought in at once. The Jewish population, which in Austria was largely concentrated in and around its capital, Vienna, was persecuted immediately after the annexation. Many Jewish men were arrested, and others were publicly humiliated by being forced to 'clean' the pavements on their hands and knees while being beaten and physically attacked. A young Jewish boy, Robert Borger, son of Erna and Leo Borger, who owned a large shop selling radios and musical instruments in Vienna, was snatched off the street by some young Nazis and locked in a synagogue. As no friendly party had witnessed what had happened and where he was, it took many hours to free him, which traumatized him to the extreme. Robert escaped Vienna with his mother in 1939, and he was fostered by a very insightful, committed Welsh couple in Caernarfon in Gwynedd. His mother had managed to obtain a position as a housekeeper and hence a visa to the UK. Robert's escape was not part of the Kindertransport scheme, but his story exemplifies the damage that the experience of persecution could do to a child. Robert continued to suffer from panic attacks after his escape to Wales: his foster parents had to take the whistle off their kettle as it reminded Robert too much of the whistles used by Nazis on the streets of Vienna. He once nearly fainted when the friendly landlord of his foster parents wanted to take him out for a walk, as he believed he was to be taken away and killed. This is just one illustration of the lasting effect that the persecution and violence had on children on the Continent.

The pogrom of 9 and 10 November 1938 perpetrated all over the German Reich (which by then included the annexed Austria) was another event which many of those who later escaped on a Kindertransport remembered. Ruth David lived with her parents and her six siblings in Fränkisch-Crumbach, a village in the rural Odenwald area of the state of Hesse in Germany. Her father owned a cigar factory which his father had founded in the nineteenth century. She remembered the terror she felt on the night of 9 and 10 November 1938, when local Nazis ransacked the factory and the family home. Ruth and Hanna fled the house and hid in the family car in terror: 'We jumped in the car and cowered together in the back. I cannot say how long we remained in our hiding place; it seemed like many hours of shivering of cold and panic. I know that what I experienced there, at the age of nine, was the greatest fear that I have ever known.'[9]

Aged 8, Wolfgang Dienemann (later William Dieneman), who escaped on a Kindertransport in January 1939 with his older sister Ursula, lived with his family in the Schöneberg district of Berlin at the time. In his later recollections of his life in Berlin, he expressed surprise that his parents sent him to school on the morning of 10 November 1938 despite what had happened the night before. When William arrived at his school, which was located right next to the then-destroyed synagogue, his teachers were surprised to see him and immediately sent him home. But William was just 8 years old, and clearly did not understand what was going on. He felt pleased that he had a day off school and decided that he would rather play with a friend than go straight home. They spent the whole day playing in the park. When William finally made his way home in the evening, his parents were beside themselves with worry, and William remembered that they were so relieved at the fact that he hadn't been harmed in the pogrom that he was not even punished for staying out without permission. His father, however, was not so lucky. When plain-clothes Gestapo officers came to the door of their flat, William's older sister Ursula truthfully told them that their father was out. Unfortunately, she was so honest that she gave them the time when he was likely to come home. The Gestapo men returned at said time and arrested him. He was beaten and tortured and incarcerated in Sachsenhausen concentration camp for some weeks. During his incarceration, he wrote a postcard to his wife, dated 20 November 1938, telling her that Ursula had to get to Bristol as fast as possible 'even if I cannot see her again before she leaves'.[10] The Dienemanns clearly had made some arrangements for the emigration of their oldest child already. Alfred Dienemann had served in the German Army in the First World War and he had connections to the UK through the Association of Jewish Ex-Servicemen (AJEX). In the end, both siblings escaped on a Kindertransport on 16 January 1939. After some months in foster families, William ended up in a boarding school in Bristol – the Avondale School – where he was lucky enough to receive a good education. His sister initially had a more difficult time in England as she was used by her foster family as a free maid and babysitter. In June 1939, the Dienemann adults also escaped to the UK, but, due to their economically difficult circumstances, William, Ursula and their parents were never able to live together as a family again – a fate that was not uncommon at all, even if the parents managed to escape to the same country as the children.

Because of its magnitude and extreme violence, the November Pogrom was widely reported on in the international media. In the UK, it sparked a reaction from a significant number of citizens, who demanded that the government should be doing something to help the persecuted Continental Jews. Their demands ultimately resulted in the visa waiver scheme for unaccompanied children that we now know as the Kindertransport.

3

Escape

Initially, the numbers of those seeking sanctuary from Nazi persecution in the UK were not very large: between 1933 and 1935, 4,500 refugees managed to find refuge in the UK, with another 5,500 arriving until early 1938.[1] Between 1933 and 1938, many sanctuary seekers preferred to flee to countries with a direct border with Germany, such as France, the Netherlands or Belgium. Austria was also seen as a country of refuge as it was obviously easier to get a job there for a German speaker. Safety in Austria turned out to be short-lived, and, for most Jewish refugees, both France and the Netherlands eventually also turned into dangerous traps rather than countries of safety. After the annexation of Austria in March 1938, the number of people trying to escape to the UK increased dramatically. In response to this development, the UK government brought in changes to its immigration procedures in April 1938 – not to make it easier to escape to the UK, but to make it harder. From April 1938, anyone who wanted to enter the UK had to be to be in possession of a visa.

Visas were only granted in very specific circumstances, mainly to those adults whose presence would be advantageous to British society or the economy. Initially, there were three ways to obtain a visa. First, the government was willing to grant visas to well-known artists and academics who would enhance the standing of the arts or academia in the UK. The psychoanalyst Sigmund Freud fell under this category. On 5 June 1938, the *Daily Mail* carried the headline: 'Freud comes to London poor and a refugee: "Here I can finish my life's work in peace."' For most artists and academics, it was a difficult, rather than an easy, route and depended on sponsorships being provided by UK institutions or patrons. Many applicants were unsuccessful, and most were in insecure positions even if they managed to be admitted to the UK.

The second category of people to be granted visas were individuals who could convince the authorities that they had the expertise and the funds to establish a business that would employ UK workers. In many cases, they were encouraged to establish a manufacturing business in one of the government's so-called 'Special Areas', which were regions in need of support because of high unemployment rates. The Schoenmann family escaped from Vienna, and the Toffler family escaped from Prague; together with fellow refugee Rudolf Wilheim, Paul Schoenmann and Hermann Toffler established the General Paper and Box Company on the Treforest Estate near Pontypridd in South Wales.[2] The paper section of the company was especially successful: it produced boxes of cigarette paper in the late 1930s and early 1940s. The business was eventually bought by the well-known cigarette-paper manufacturer Rizla in 1946.

The third category of refugees who had a chance of being granted a visa for the UK were those who were willing to work in domestic service, and able to find a position in a UK household. Over 20,000 refugees, mainly women, escaped via this scheme. Since the 1920s, it had become increasingly difficult for households in the UK to find domestic staff due to the poor wages and difficult working conditions, such as the long hours and the requirement to live in their employers' household.

Unsurprisingly, British working-class women preferred different jobs that were opening up in manufacturing and the retail sector. The country was said to be suffering from a 'servant crisis'. Admitting refugees on so-called 'domestic service permits' was seen as alleviating this labour shortage and aiding the smooth running of British households. However, many of the large number of women who found positions as maids, housekeepers or cooks, and the smaller number of men who accepted employment as butlers or gardeners, were not experienced in domestic service. In fact, it was not uncommon that those desperate to escape from persecution took positions despite the fact that their only experience of domestic labour was as employers of domestic staff rather than as the ones who actually carried out the work. Many amusing anecdotes exist about misunderstandings regarding expectations of this sort of employment arrangement.[3] Continental Jewish organizations set up courses to prepare the potential domestics for their role, and the Central Office for Refugees in the UK issued a leaflet in 1940 entitled 'Mistress and maid: general information for the use of domestic refugees and their employers', which instructed the refugee domestics on how to behave in their new positions: 'it is good manners to speak and walk quietly, both in the house and in the street and public places. You will notice that the mistress usually states her requirements in the form of a request. This should be carried out at once as an order. It is not correct to argue with a mistress.' There were a small number of other sectors, such as psychiatric nursing and some agricultural jobs, that were considered to be suffering from a labour shortage and in which it was possible to obtain a visa if you could find employment and submit the right paperwork. Eventually, the fourth category of refugees who were allowed to find sanctuary in the UK were, of course, unaccompanied child refugees who came via the Kindertransport scheme, which was in fact a visa waiver scheme. Those under 18 who were admitted to the UK for education or training purposes did not need a visa.

The first three categories outlined above clearly show that the government's policies were not first and foremost guided by altruistic principles and the desire to save as many persecuted people as possible. By and large, it can be said that rescuing people from persecution was only supported if there was an advantage (or at least no disadvantage) by doing so. Ideally, the refugee had to bring an advantage to UK society. The refugees should not be a financial burden on the state; nor should they compete with UK citizens on the labour market.

These regulations led to a situation in which many of those desperately seeking refuge were refused entry to the UK. Despite these strict criteria, it is estimated that a further 50,000 refugees arrived between the annexation of Austria in March 1938 and the start of the Second World War in September 1939. In some cases, the officials who were in charge of granting visas were more lenient than in other cases and bent the rules somewhat. One extreme example is Frank Foley, who worked as a passport officer at the British Embassy in Berlin, and is said to have saved many lives by issuing entry documents to people who should not have had them according to the letter of the law. In other cases, the applicants were economical with the truth. Fanny Höchstetter was a 30-year-old former civil servant from southern Germany. When she applied for a domestic service permit in order to take up a position as a maid, she used a reference from her uncle which praised her housekeeping experience and skills. In reality, Fanny detested housework and had little experience. After arriving in the UK, she did not get on well with her employer and felt that she was being treated like a skivvy. After the start of the war, the regulation that domestic permit holders had to stay with their sponsoring employer was amended, and such refugees were allowed to change the type of their employment and their employer. Fanny quit her domestic service position and ended up working as a chambermaid in a hotel in Llangollen. This she preferred, and she stayed there for the rest of the war, marrying a fellow refugee and starting a family.[4]

As discussed, the government was put under pressure from the public after the pogrom that saw widespread state-sponsored violence on 9 and 10 November 1938 in the German Reich. The Quakers had been assisting refugees since the Nazi takeover in Germany, and had sent a delegation to Germany to find out what could be done to help the persecuted Jews. Upon their return, this delegation met with the prime minister, and so did representatives of the Anglo-Jewish community. At a Cabinet Committee Meeting on Foreign Policy on 14 November 1938, various possible reactions to the events were discussed, and Prime Minister Neville Chamberlain stated that 'something effective should be done to alleviate the terrible fate of the Jews in Germany'.[5] He alluded to the public mood, and that there was a certain pressure on the government to be seen to be doing something. However, although various suggestions for helping the German Jews to leave Germany were discussed, none was decided on during this particular meeting. The next day, a group of Anglo-Jewish leaders met with Prime Minister Chamberlain, and at this meeting the idea of temporarily admitting a number of unaccompanied children for the purpose of training and education was discussed. Just a week later, the Home Secretary, Sir Samuel Hoare, announced the government's new refugee policy, which included the directive that all children whose maintenance could be guaranteed by private individuals or charitable organizations were allowed to be admitted to Britain without going through the arduous process of applying for a visa. This was the official go-ahead for the Kindertransport.[6]

The issue was debated in the House of Commons on 21 November 1938 as a government proposal on the subject of 'Refugees'. It is striking how Chamberlain did not even consider committing the government to helping refugees, but

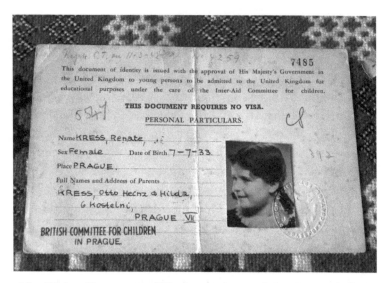

Visa Waiver Document of Kindertransport refugee Renate Collins
With permission from Amy Daniel

stated that the ability to assist those in need was limited to the ability of voluntary organizations to manage and finance assistance for the persecuted:

> With regard to the United Kingdom, the number of refugees which Great Britain can agree to admit, either for a temporary stay or for permanent settlement, is limited by the capacity of the voluntary organisations dealing with the refugee problem to undertake the responsibility for selecting, receiving and maintaining a further number of refugees. His Majesty's Government are keeping in close touch with the Committee which has been set up to co-ordinate the activities of the voluntary organisations engaged upon this task.[7]

The matter was debated more concretely in an evening debate, and the Labour MP Philip Noel-Baker, who was a Quaker, pointed out that the task was too great to be undertaken by charitable organizations and argued that the government should at least provide loans: 'Private charity cannot solve the problem now. The Government need not be alarmed at the prospect of guaranteeing loans.'[8] In response, Conservative MP William Butcher voiced the fear that it would be problematic if refugees were admitted who were reliant on government funds or would compete with British citizens on the labour market. He also stated that it should not be the most in need that should be given priority, but those most able to be of benefit to the UK:

> We must, of necessity, select those whom we are most able to help. They could be selected from age groups capable of being self-supporting over a considerable period of years, and most likely to become loyal citizens in the ultimate country of their adoption. Good character should be one pre-requisite and robust good health another. Thirdly, there should be some technical skill . . . lest there should be a tremendous influx into this country of refugees who are unable to maintain themselves and who would have to compete with our own citizens for a livelihood. After all, many of our own people are hard put to it to find work and a means of livelihood.[9]

This is echoed by other contributors to the debate. At 9.35 p.m. that evening, the Home Secretary Sir Samuel Hoare made the statement that the government felt that the UK could manage to admit children 'with whom we could deal in large numbers, provided they were sponsored by responsible bodies and responsible individuals', again emphasizing that the responsibility, both pastoral and financial, was not to be shouldered by the government. Hoare elaborated further, essentially giving the go-ahead for the Kindertransport that facilitated visa-free entry for minors:

> So also with these Jewish and non-Aryan children, I believe that we could find homes in this country for a very large number

without any harm to our own population. The Co-ordinating Committee and the other organisations told me that they would be prepared to bring over here all the children whose maintenance could be guaranteed, either by their funds or by generous individuals, and that all that will probably be necessary will be for the Home Office . . . to facilitate their entry into this country. . . . . Here is a chance of taking the young generation of a great people, here is a chance of mitigating to some extent the terrible sufferings of their parents and their friends.[10]

It is interesting to note that Hoare stressed in his speech that the child refugees were the young generation of a great people, a value judgement that might have influenced later selection policies – that is, the fact that the organizers in the UK were very keen to admit only children who were considered fully physically and mentally healthy.

To admit only the children, and not their parents and families, is clearly one of the most controversial aspects of the Kindertransport. It has sometimes been suggested that parting from your own children was seen as more normal and less painful at that time. There are certainly more examples of children growing up outside their birth families in informal fostering arrangements in the first half of the twentieth century. It has also been suggested that, as it was normal for the British upper middle class to send their children to boarding school, this might have led members of the political elite in the UK at the time to believe that separating children and their parents was not as traumatic as it turned out to be. It is therefore interesting to see that Hoare mentioned the pain that the parents were likely to experience in his speech the very evening the government gave the go-ahead for the Kindertransport scheme:

I could not help thinking what a terrible dilemma it was to the Jewish parents in Germany to have to choose between sending their children to a foreign country, into the unknown, and continuing to live in the terrible conditions to which they are now reduced in Germany. I saw this morning one of the representatives of the Quaker organisations, who told me that he had only arrived in England this morning from a visit to Germany and a visit to Holland. He inquired of the Jewish organisations in Germany what would be the attitude of the Jewish parents to a proposal of this kind, and he told me that the Jewish parents were almost unanimously in favour of facing this parting with their children and taking the risks of their children going to a foreign country, rather than keeping them with them to face the unknown dangers with which they are faced in Germany.[11]

Many of the parents in the persecuted Continental families decided that they would part from their children if it was the only way to get them to safety. However, many also thought that the separation would not be very long, and sometimes the parents tried to put their children on a Kindertransport to keep the family together. For those who had managed to find a position in domestic service, the Israelitische Kultusgemeinde Wien (IKG) had pre-printed application forms on which parents could state that they had obtained a domestic permit to enter the UK and thus wished their child to be considered for a Kindertransport.[12] This shows that parents wanted their children to be in the same country as them at least, possibly hoping for a speedy reunion. This worked out for some families, but in the case of most of those who did work as domestic staff, their employers saw them as employees first and foremost, and were not sensitive to their situation. Most were not allowed to have their children live with them. In other cases, living as a family was equally impossible: the economically difficult circumstances and limited accommodation dictated that child refugees could not live with their parents, even if they had all resettled in Britain.[13]

Refugee children inevitably experience a separation from familiar environments – after already experiencing oppression and persecution. It is therefore obvious that separating them from their parents and families will add to their trauma. Hedwig Mosbacher considered trying to escape to the UK via the domestic visa route, but this did not work out, and she and her husband Otto saw no possibility of him being granted a visa for the UK. Despite ending up with loving and supportive foster carers, Eva clearly missed her parents very much and continued to express her wish to be reunited in her letters.

While, undoubtedly, some individual UK politicians at various times acted out of humanitarian concern for the persecuted Jewish population of the German Reich, the overall government policy was guided by a cost–benefit analysis that did not see providing sanctuary for refugees as its most important aim.

The family of Ruth David is an example that shows us the complex journeys made by different members of the family – in this case, the six siblings – to safety. Ruth's parents ultimately were not able to escape and were murdered in the Holocaust. Ruth's father and oldest brother Ernst were assaulted during the November Pogrom and incarcerated in Buchenwald. Ernst was released quickly because he already had a visa for the USA. Their father's release was much slower. After 1933, the family had planned the emigration of the younger adults: Ernst to the USA, and Werner to Argentina. Werner had undergone training in agriculture to be accepted. By the end of 1938, both Ernst and Werner managed to emigrate, and immediately started to look for ways to get the rest of the family to safety. Ruth and her sister Hannah then escaped on a Kindertransport. Ruth was placed in a children's home in Tynemouth, and then another one in the Lake District which was run by a matron and a cook who were both refugees themselves. She recalled the difficulties of the children's situation, and how some of the child refugees were treated badly and beaten by the adults in charge. Ruth's youngest siblings, Michael and Feodora, stayed with the parents. It is not too difficult to understand how the different paths were chosen for the siblings, according to their age and maturity and their ability to live without parental support. The overall plan was for them all to escape to the USA or Argentina – the latter seemed the more promising destination as it did not have the same strict quota system as the USA. Extensive correspondence between the different family members has survived. In March 1940, the father wrote to Werner, clearly believing that their joint emigration – the plan was to pick up Hanna and Ruth from England en route to Argentina – was still a strong possibility.[14] However, Ruth's parents were deported to France together with the two youngest children. Mother Margarete and the two youngest children managed to escape, and Michael and Feodora survived by being hidden with a false identity in France. Margarete joined her husband Moritz in the Camp des Milles, and both were moved to Drancy, and from there deported to Auschwitz on 17 August 1942, where they were murdered. In this way, all six siblings survived, but their parents did not, and the siblings' lives took a completely different path and all six had very different experiences.

How did the children feel when their families decided that they should part and the children should escape unaccompanied on a Kindertransport? Because of the threats experienced, most older children understood their parents' efforts to find a way for them to emigrate, even if they were scared to leave their families. Martha Immerdauer (later Martha Blend) was born in 1930 and only 9 years old when she fled from Vienna to the UK. She remembered both her anxiety and the reasons for leaving her family:

When my parents broke this news to me, I was devastated and burst into hysterical sobs at the mere thought. . . . I felt as though some force stronger than myself was dragging me into an abyss and I had no power to prevent it. Although I was still very young, I had seen and understood the build-up of terror in the last two years, so I knew very well that my parents were doing this out of sheer necessity.[15]

Researching the life stories of former Kindertransportees from interviews and memoirs shows that many were told by their parents that the parents would follow them to Britain, or emigrate themselves and send for the children after a period of a few months' separation. Some children were placated with unrealistic promises or even told that they were just going on a holiday. This was the case with Anne and Horst Marschner – discussed in more detail in the next chapter – whose mother told them that she would be coming to see them in two weeks' time, and whose headmaster told them that they were just going on a holiday. Although it seems likely that this was told to the children to alleviate their anxiety about being separated from their families, letters from the parents show that in many cases they did, in fact, try to organize onward migration to a third country where the whole family would then be reunited. Milena Roth escaped as a 6-year-old from Czechoslovakia. Her birth mother wrote to her foster carer in English, dated 3 June 1939:

> I feel awfully grateful and excited. . . . And please tell your husband, that both my husband and I, thank you for your great kindness. I feel perfectly sure Milena will be safe in your hands and it is really for the moment the best for her. Let us hope that it will not take a too long time and that we all three, Milena, my husband and I can soon live together.[16]

Even if the children's escape was well organized, there was no guarantee that they wouldn't find the experience traumatic. But, in some cases, the children were not at all prepared for their flight and had little or no idea what was going on. Kärry Wertheim (later Ellen Davis) was born in 1929 into an

Orthodox Jewish family in Germany.[17] The initial selection of suitable candidates for a Kindertransport was made by the German and Austrian Jewish communities in the case of Jewish children, or the local Quaker or Christian partners in the case of those families who were persecuted as Jewish but did not define themselves as Jewish. But it was normally the parents or guardians who had to apply for the scheme in the first place. It seems that Orthodox parents were less open to the idea of letting their children flee as unaccompanied minors, possibly due to the significant role the birth family plays in Orthodox Judaism. Additionally, the UK organizing committee, eventually called the Refugee Children's Movement, were not able to guarantee foster placements in Orthodox families. They were even unable to guarantee foster placements in Jewish families. The large majority of foster families who volunteered to take care of a child refugee were not Jewish. The IKG asked the birth parents to sign a permission form to enable their children to be fostered by Christian families. This diminished the chances of selection for a Kindertransport for the children of Orthodox families who wanted their children to grow up within their faith. Some Orthodox Jewish children managed to flee on a Kindertransport as part of an Orthodox group which then stayed together after their arrival in the UK. Some Orthodox children did end up with Orthodox foster parents, as was the case with Ellen Davis.

Ellen grew up in a large Orthodox Jewish family as the oldest of six siblings. Her very early childhood was idyllic, mainly spent in a large house and garden in a rural location with her mother and her father, her maternal grandparents, and one aunt and five uncles. They lived in Hoof, a small village located on the main route to the city of Kassel in the state of Hesse in western Germany. Ellen's grandfather was a *Shochet*, a butcher who slaughters animals according to Jewish religious law. Together with his sons, he either sold the meat in the small shop attached to their house or travelled to the city of Kassel to sell it at a market. Ellen's grandmother is described by her as a large kind woman with white hair and a white pinafore who organized the house, comforted the children, cooked, baked, and lit the Shabbat meal candles every Saturday.

The large family lived the traditional life of a religious Jewish family, a life in which the men dominated the lives of the women. Ellen was the first child of her young mother and father, and another sibling was born every year after her birth, despite the fact that her mother suffered from debilitating varicose veins while pregnant. Ellen took on the role of a young carer. As the oldest daughter, Ellen looked after her siblings as soon as they were born, and also looked after her mother when she was ill during her pregnancies. The grandfather was the head of the extended family and made decisions on all matters in public and in the home, and expected obedience from all members of the family. Ellen's father Julius was clearly an independent and somewhat rogue member of the family. He had mainly non-Jewish friends and he only joined his in-laws and his wife in the synagogue on high holidays. He did not work for the family business. Instead, he was keen on sport, boxing and bodybuilding, and spent a lot of time outside the home.

Before 1933, the family was well liked in the village and interacted with their non-Jewish neighbours in a cooperative and friendly manner. They joined in with communal activities. Ellen and her siblings played with the other children in the village. However, Ellen describes how after January 1933 the other children's behaviour changed suddenly; some of them shouted swear words at her and excluded her from their games.

When Ellen was 5, she had joined the two-room village school. As is customary in Germany, on her first day she received a large cardboard cone filled with sweets, and like many children Ellen was excited to experience this rite of passage. But by 1934 the Nazi flag with the swastika was raised in the schoolyard, and the non-Jewish children and the teachers would no longer interact with the Jewish minority. Ellen and the small number of other Jewish children were forced to sit at the back of the class and ordered to stay in the classroom during break time.

When Ellen's grandfather's butchery business had to cease trading, it led to him looking to leave Germany, despite the facts that his family had lived in the village of Hoof since 1760 and that he had fought for Germany in the First World War. The grandparents managed to obtain a visa for emigration to Argentina. They then had to pay for the passage immediately because there were not many places left on one of the passenger ships. This they did and they left quickly, and without the rest of the family. The grandparents planned to establish themselves, open a new business and save some money, and then enable their children and grandchildren to join them, when they could afford it and when they had obtained further visas. But, unfortunately, this proved impossible. The departure of the grandparents clearly had a negative effect on the family members left behind. Without them, the rest of the family struggled financially and, surrounded by a largely hostile village community, things quickly deteriorated for them in Hoof. In December 1937, when a group of Hitler Youth violently attacked the synagogue in the village, Ellen, her sister Ruth, and her brothers Rolf, Heinz and Sally, were sent to the Jewish Orphanage in the nearby large town of Kassel in the hope that they would receive support and safety there.

Unfortunately, this move did not provide them with a safer upbringing. As in many other towns, the well-known location of Jewish orphanages acted as a magnet for those intending to perpetrate violence against Jews. This meant that the children and their adult carers were always fearful of attacks and only rarely ventured out. In the orphanage, Ellen continued in her role as oldest child, carer and protector of her siblings. Funding for the orphanage was also virtually non-existent. Moreover, by 1938, it was illegal for Jews to buy food in non-Jewish shops. Seeing how everyone in the orphanage was hungry, 9-year-old

Ellen and her brother Rolf, aged 8, volunteered to go shopping
for the orphanage. They managed to do this for two months
without incident. Eventually, however, they were attacked by
a group of Hitler Youth and beaten up. Ellen suffered kidney
damage, which had a detrimental effect on her for the rest of
her life.

After this incident and an arson attack during the November
Pogrom, the supervisor at the orphanage arranged for the
children to be considered for a Kindertransport to the UK.
All the children's photographs were taken for selection purposes, and it was Ellen who was eventually chosen. Ellen later
remembered how her father appeared one day out of the blue,
in an emaciated state and with a shaven head. He took her to
various offices for papers to be signed, which must have been
her application for a place on a Kindertransport. Ellen later
recalled that she was not given any explanation at all. She was
able to say a brief goodbye to both her parents and her youngest brother Ludwig, and then driven to a train station to start
her journey to the UK.

It is very difficult to imagine how bewildering this experience must have been for Ellen. She had never been separated
from her siblings. She had never been on a train before; in fact,
she had never even seen a train before. She had spent the first
ten years of her life in circumstances that prevented her from
venturing far from her family, her village, and later the orphanage. She had never seen the sea before, did not know how ships
or ferries worked, and had certainly never left Germany. When
she tried to remember the journey years later, Ellen stated
that she had very little recollection of the detail and told an
anecdote that she had tried to eat a banana without peeling
it because she had never even seen one before. This complete
bewilderment continued when she was picked up in London
by her foster father, who took her on yet another train. This
time it was a train to Swansea. She did not understand any
English of course, and when the conductor shouted the name

of the destination of the train on the platform, she did not know that this was the name of where it was headed. She later described this moment of incomprehension and confusion:

> WHAT WAS SWANSEA? As we entered the train in London, I heard a man, as he wandered up and down outside, shouting Swansea, Swansea. I had no idea what he was saying, but I was struck by the word and the funny voice he had. When our long journey ended, there was another man shouting Swansea. He sounded very different. So again, what was Swansea?[18]

The town with the bewildering name was to become her home and she still lived there in 2023.

In August 1939, Ellen received a postcard from her mother announcing that Ellen now had a new baby sister called Zilla. After that, there were no more communications, as receiving mail from the Continent was very difficult after the outbreak of war. Ellen's father managed to escape Germany, was interned as an Enemy Alien on the Isle of Man, and even managed to visit her in Swansea several times, before being deported to Australia. Ellen's mother, her brothers Rolf, Heinz, Sally and Ludwig, and her sisters Ruth and Zilla, were deported on one of the first transports to Riga where they were murdered. The only memento of her family that was left for Ellen to keep for the rest of her life was a photograph of herself in Hoof with her mother and all of her siblings, bar the youngest.

The Kindertransport organized from Czechoslovakia and Poland took place a few months after the first ones organized from Germany and Austria. In October 1938, the German Reich had annexed the Sudetenland, the part of Czechoslovakia with a majority ethnic German population. Most Jewish residents of this area left and resettled in the part of Czechoslovakia that was not under German jurisdiction. However, when the German Reich annexed further territory and Hitler proclaimed the Protectorate of Bohemia and Moravia from Prague Castle, many Jewish families were urgently seeking an escape route to safety away from their country of origin. They had the same difficulties as the German and Austrian families in obtaining visas and permits, and were possibly under more pressure than the families in Germany, who had had longer to prepare. Most could not find refuge as a family easily.

The Kindertransports from Prague were organized in a slightly different manner from the ones from Germany and Austria. There was a group of British citizens who were living, or at least temporarily staying, in Prague and who were trying to facilitate the escape of persecuted, Jewish and non-Jewish, Czechoslovaks. Doreen Warriner ran the offices of the British Committee for Refugees from Czechoslovakia (BCRC) in the city. During the Christmas period of 1938, she was joined by two men from the UK, Martin Blake and Nicholas Winton. The men had originally planned to go skiing with a school group from Westminster School where Blake worked. However, Blake cancelled his trip and travelled to Prague instead to help out the BCRC. Winton then decided to follow his friend and was instrumental in setting up bringing refugee children from Czechoslovakia to the UK. In the end, 669 child refugees managed to flee on a Kindertransport from Prague. These transports were organized using the Kindertransport scheme but there were some differences in procedure, and they were obviously facilitated by a different group of helpers.

Numerically speaking, the smallest group of Kindertransport refugees came from Poland. One group of children came from the Free City of Danzig (today Gdansk). This group of child refugees arrived in the usual way on the train and via the Hook of Holland to Harwich. Three further groups of altogether 150 minors arrived in 1939 aboard the packet steamer *Warszawa* from Gdynia in Poland. Their escape was arranged by the Polish Jewish Refugee Fund and they came from a refugee camp on the Polish–German border where conditions were extremely desperate.

This refugee camp had been set up due to a relatively little-known event in October 1938 called the 'Polenaktion' (Polish Action) carried out by Germany. It constituted the first deportation of a large number of Jews instigated by the German Reich. The Nazi government had detained and arrested around 17,000 Polish Jews living in Germany on 28 October 1938 with the aim of deporting them to Poland.[19] The immediate reason for this move was the Nazis' fear that the Polish government was about to withdraw Polish citizenship from Jewish Polish citizens who had been living abroad for a length of time, and that the German Reich would then be 'lumbered' with them. Most of those arrested were deported immediately to Poland and crossed the German–Polish border. Some, however, who arrived at the border crossing of Zbąszyń, were not allowed to enter Poland. Over 8,000 people were then effectively stuck in no man's land near the border town of Zbąszyń – where a refugee camp was established in an abandoned flour mill and some stables – and the German border. This group of displaced people were in a dire situation, lacking almost everything, including food and medicine. In response to this humanitarian disaster, the Polish Jewish Refugee Fund was formed in the UK, and, apart from sending aid to the border area, the Fund also organized for some children and young people to join a Kindertransport.

It is clear that, from 1938, the situation of Jews on the Continent was becoming more and more difficult. Larger numbers sought to escape to Britain, and the fear of these large numbers of sanctuary seekers worried the British government, and motivated them to implement more restrictive regulations. The special arrangements made for providing sanctuary for persecuted Continental refugees were not guided first and foremost by humanitarian principles, and the policies did not give priority to those most in need. Rather, they were aimed at admitting groups and individuals who would be of benefit to the UK, or at least who would not disturb the status quo unduly or demand too much organizational or financial assistance from the UK government. The underage refugees who fled via the Kindertransport scheme were not likely to compete with UK citizens on the labour market, in the very near future at least. In fact, a lot of them received a stamp on the back of their child's identity document that said in capital letters: 'LEAVE TO LAND GRANTED ON THIS DAY ON THE CONDITION THAT THE HOLDER DOES NOT ENTER INTO ANY EMPLOYMENT PAID OR UNPAID WHILE IN THE UNITED KINGDOM.'[20] The second stipulation for the organization of the Kindertransport was that financial and organizational support should be borne by volunteers and charities and not by the UK government. This attitude was to influence the shape and form of the Kindertransport, and the lives of Kindertransport refugees for years to come.

4

Organization

There were several diverse organizations that made use of the Kindertransport scheme to get children out of harm's way and helped to organize the individual transports. There were two large Jewish organizations, in Berlin and Vienna, that acted as conduits for the application process from these areas, as well as smaller Christian organizations and the Quakers. The Children's section of the BCRC acted to get child refugees out of Prague, and the London-based Polish Jewish Refugee Fund (PJRF) organized four transports from the Polish–German border area. There were also some smaller organizations that made use of the scheme: several German schools used the Kindertransport scheme to relocate their students to the UK, and Zionist organizations used it to bring teenagers to the UK, intending for them to prepare to emigrate to Palestine. On the UK side, the umbrella organization was the Movement for the Care of Children from Germany, which was later renamed the Refugee Children's Movement (RCM). Under the RCM umbrella, there were local committees in different areas of the UK who organized the work on the ground.

Organizing the Kindertransport was a monumental task for all concerned: the organizing bodies on the Continent, the committees in the UK and all their staff and volunteers. The surviving archives show an extensive correspondence between the different parts of the operation.[1] This task was undertaken while the Nazis were unrelenting in their persecution and exclusion of the Jewish population in the German Reich, and was made more difficult by the lack of government backing in organizational and financial terms in the UK. This led to untrained individuals making decisions in an atmosphere that can often only be described as hostile. Child refugees who made it to the UK had to 'prove' that they were worth saving. The way the different organizations interacted with each other and the decentralized system, which had little professional input and not enough funding, also led to an approach that was focused on managing and administrating the scheme and did not meet the needs of individual children.

As discussed, the eruption of violence towards the Jewish population in Germany during the November Pogroms of 1938 not only was a turning point for German and Austrian Jewish organizations and individuals, but also showed the international community that the German Jews were in a desperate situation. The speed of organization and sheer scale of the Kindertransport scheme are two of the reasons why the scheme is often mentioned with admiration; these facts are also cited as arguments for the uniqueness of the scheme. However, this assessment regarding both points needs qualification because there were precedents for the swiftly organized immigration to Britain of both large numbers of people and children. During the First World War, a large number of Belgian refugees were admitted to the UK, while during the Spanish Civil War about 4,000 unaccompanied Basque children were taken in. Other very similar schemes to different European countries were also developed. For example, the Kindertransport to Sweden, which admitted 500 child refugees, was set up in a similar way to the one to the UK.[2]

The organization of the actual Kindertransport certainly happened in a short space of time: there were less than two weeks between the go-ahead for the UK Kindertransport scheme and the first transport arriving in the UK on 2 December 1938. This would not have been possible, however, if both the Continental organization and the organizers on the British side had not had some experience. On the German side, a Department for Child Emigration (Abteilung Kinderauswanderung der Reichsvertretung der Deutschen Juden) had already been established by the German Board of Jewish Deputies in 1933. This meant that there were people with experience available who could deal with the formalities and organization of a large group of Jewish children to be sent to the UK. In Austria, the situation was slightly different, as there had been no communal initiative to send unaccompanied children abroad before the annexation of Austria in March 1938, which made the helpers less experienced. The fact that the Jewish population in Austria was concentrated mainly in Vienna made their challenge a little easier in this respect – in comparison with Germany, where there were many rural Jewish communities. The offices of the Child Welfare Department (Jugendfürsorge-Abteilung) of the IKG – the Jewish Community in Vienna – were in charge of the Kindertransport from the former Austrian territory. From June 1938, three months after the annexation, a scheme for Emigration of Minors had been organized between the IKG and several countries, including Sweden and the UK. There was a list of 546 older children with fully prepared applications ready to emigrate without their families by summer 1938. Social workers from the IKG had assessed their cases and written a positive report, and their parents had given consent. However, only 29 had successfully managed to find safety abroad. We know more details about the organization of the transports from Vienna than the ones from German cities because the archives of the Board of Deputies in Berlin were largely destroyed, whereas the archives of the IKG have survived, as did the archives of the Christian organizations in Berlin. This makes a reconstruction of the workings of the latter organizations much easier, but from the fragments that have survived from Berlin, it is reasonable to assume that Jewish operations from there would have functioned similarly to those from Vienna.

About 20 per cent of the children were not processed under the auspices of the Jewish organization as the families did not consider themselves Jewish but were defined as such by the Nazi Race Laws; as discussed, according to these laws a person was considered Jewish if they had one Jewish grandparent. This did not correspond to the Jewish community's definition, of course, nor to many individuals' self-definition. At the time, this group were described as so-called 'non-Aryan Christians' by both British and German organizations and included children with a combination of Christian and Jewish parents, or grandparents who either had no religious affiliation or were in fact Christians. The Quakers, also known as the Society of Friends, and organizations connected to the Protestant and Catholic Churches on the Continent assisted this group of children.[3] The RCM in the UK was an interdenominational organization and took care of all the child refugees, no matter what their background. Not unsurprisingly, a certain amount of wrangling is reported to have taken place between the representatives of the different groups about the numbers of places allocated to each group. The Department for Child Emigration of the Board of Deputies, the Christian organizations, which also had their offices in Berlin, and the IKG collected applications from Jewish organizations and community offices located all over the German Reich It is not easy to tell one universally valid story of the organization of the Kindertransport as there were small differences and inconsistencies regarding the selection criteria, for example, but also regarding how the transports were organized and how and where placements were found in the UK. My aim is to give a general picture while acknowledging some of the differing experiences undergone by those who fled through this complex scheme.

The first individual Kindertransport from the German Reich started from Berlin on 1 December 1938 and arrived in Harwich on 2 December 1938. The first transport from Vienna left on 10 December. The transports from all areas of Germany and the former Austria helped over 9,500 children to flee persecution and come to the UK. The transports arranged from Prague, which helped 669 children find sanctuary in the UK, were organized by the Child Emigration section of the BCRC, and the first one destined for the UK left on 14 March 1939. The BCRC organizer Doreen Warriner put Nicholas Winton in charge of the child refugee section after he had helped out at the office in Prague for only a few days. In fact, he was on a fortnight's holiday and had to ask his boss for more time off to be able to follow through what would clearly be an important task. Neither Warriner nor Winton knew much about the newly established Kindertransport. In fact, Winton sent a letter to his mother back in London and asked her to clarify certain regulations with the Home Office for him: 'I have another job which may be difficult. Can you go to the Immigration Section of the Home Office and find out what guarantees are needed to bring a child into the country?'[4] Around 154 Kindertransport refugees fled from the border region between the German Reich and Poland between 14 February 1939 and late August 1939. Most of the Kindertransport refugees from Poland travelled by sea on the *Warszawa*; there are some iconic photographs of them disembarking in London.

To be able to be considered for a Kindertransport, the parents or guardians of the children had to get in touch with the relevant organization that administered applications in that locality. Despite the urgency at the time, this was a fundamentally bureaucratic process. For example, an information sheet issued for 'non-Aryan' German children stated that each application needed to consist of three copies of a completed

Kindertransport refugees on the *Warszawa*
Bundesarchiv, Germany

questionnaire, four to six passport photographs, one medi-
cal report from a physician who had examined the child and
found him or her to be healthy and not suffering from any
'communicable diseases or psychiatric illnesses', and a one-
page justification of the urgency of the application.[5] The IKG
demanded similar documents. The Continental organizations
collected the applications, checked whether all documents
were complete, potentially demanded more or different documents and then pre-selected the applications and sent the ones
they considered most urgent on to London, where they were
received by the RCM. Its headquarters were located first in
Bloomsbury House in London, and later evacuated to Surrey.
Here the applications were assessed again and the children
who were deemed to be suitable for refuge in the UK were
chosen. This was then communicated back to the Department
for Child Emigration, the IKG or one of the other Continental
organizing bodies.

If successful, the children and their parents were subsequently informed of the decision. Those who were successful and were allowed to join a Kindertransport were notified of their likely departure date. They were allowed to take two small pieces of luggage, which had to be labelled and had to be light enough for the children to carry them themselves. Most children also had a label attached to their clothing, which is often shown in photographs of the Kindertransport. No valuables and only a small amount of money were allowed to be taken out of the German Reich. The age limit for applicants was initially 17, but this was lowered to 16 as some applicants turned 18 while on the waiting list for a Kindertransport and therefore became ineligible under the scheme. To avoid this complication, the age limit was lowered in early 1939.

One major requirement was the £50 guarantee that had to be given to indemnify the UK government against any costs that might arise from admitting the child to the UK. Initially, the guarantor had to sign a written undertaking 'declaring that, being possessed of sufficient means, I undertake fully to provide for and maintain said child until he/she reaches the age of eighteen years'.[6] This was clearly not something that those on low incomes could do. From 1 March 1939, the guarantor system was made more severe by the fact that now the government demanded that the guarantors deposited the £50 into a blocked government bank account. On 17 March 1939, Colonel Josiah Wedgwood MP called it a tax on 'charitable minded people' and 'prohibitive' in a debate in the House of Commons. The Home Secretary Sir Samuel Hoare replied that 'the financial position of the Movement is now such that if provision is to be made for more children, it is necessary for the Movement to find guarantors'.[7] The government again declined to step up and assist the child refugees financially.

Additionally, funds were needed for the actual journey and the upkeep of the children. Some of the child refugees' birth parents were in a position to pay for the travel costs and the initial maintenance, or had relatives or friends in the UK who could do so; however, most were not. Eleanor Rathbone, another MP who championed the cause of refugees, argued in a pamphlet published in 1939 that private charitable appeals would not be sufficient to raise the necessary funds.[8] She argued that several million pounds were required and should be provided by the government.

One major source of funds was the Anglo-Jewish community's pre-existing Jewish Refugee Committee. During the 1930s, the committee raised over £5 million for Continental refugees. Another source of funding was the Lord Baldwin Fund for Refugees. Philip Voss, a Jewish barrister and Labour Party activist, was a prime mover in the foundation of this charity. He persuaded Lord Baldwin, the former British prime minister, to lend his name to the Fund and speak out on behalf of the cause. In early December 1938, Baldwin launched an appeal on BBC radio in aid of this new charity, and advertisements were placed in newspapers.[9] Baldwin outlined how Jewish children, and those of Jewish descent, in Germany and Austria faced an existential threat and proclaimed 'Shall they live? Before it is too late get them out!', a headline that was also used for the newspaper advertising for the Baldwin Fund. Other prominent individuals, such as the Archbishop of Canterbury, Dr Cosmo Lang and the Roman Catholic Cardinal Archbishop Arthur Hinsley, gave their support to the charity. The Post Office Savings Bank issued special savings stamp books in support of the appeal. Many newspapers, even those like the *Daily Mail* that had a long history of animosity towards offering refugees sanctuary in the UK, supported the Fund, which raised over £500,000 within six months.[10]

Half of the money was used to finance the immigration and maintenance costs of Jewish child refugees. Other guarantees were provided by individuals and other charities. Some individual guarantors were private individuals, who were identical with the child's foster carers. This was the case, for example, with 8-year old Lia Blum (later Lia Lesser) who was fostered by an English teacher from Ynys Môn who also put up the guarantee.[11] Other individuals or organizations just guaranteed the upkeep of the child refugee while the child was placed elsewhere: for example, the guarantee for the very young Thomas Beerman (later Tom Berman) was raised by the Jewish Weekly Appeal Fund in London, but he was fostered by a Mrs S. K. Miller in Glasgow. The guarantee for Anneliese Adler was raised by the Woodcraft Folk in Tooting, but she was fostered by a Mrs Merritt Oldland near Bristol. Until about March 1939, an unspecified number of children who were sent to Britain did not have an individual guarantor, be that a person or an individual organization, but were guaranteed by the RCM as part of a large 'pool guarantee'. Due to financial constraints, by spring 1939 this pool of guarantees from general funds was restricted to 200 cases, which meant that only if 1 of the 200 individuals was no longer in need of a guarantee from the RCM could another child refugee come to Britain using that guarantee in his or her stead. From March 1939 onwards, generally only children who had an individual guarantor could enter Britain. This was a significant change in procedure and led to an even more complicated relationship between the Continental organizations and the RCM.

The Continental organizers were under pressure from the parents and families to get as many children as possible who had applied for the Kindertransport scheme on a train to the UK. They also had daily experience of persecution and its consequences. From the files of the IKG, we can see that amongst those whom they tried to get on a Kindertransport were children whose fathers were incarcerated in concentration camps or those whose families had lost their homes or were destitute. In some cases, the IKG were already supporting these families with small welfare payments. Their volunteers and employees tried to prioritize the most urgent cases. Many reports on the family situation of a child mentioned the families' destitute circumstances. The archives hold extensive correspondence with parents and family members who were trying to enquire about the progress of applications.

The Christian organizations in Berlin received similar correspondence. Their information leaflet included a section on 'Timeframe of application' which stated in no uncertain terms that repeated enquiry from parents was endangering the smooth running of the organization, and that parents should not do this and should wait to be contacted. At the same time, the political situation was worsening, and the persecution intensifying. On the UK side, the RCM only had limited financial means to put up new guarantees, pay for other costs and actually find placements for the children. The UK organizers felt the pressure from the Continental side, and this is borne out by an extensive correspondence which sometimes could get quite terse: 'The Movement for the Transport of Children, again, cannot bring over more unguaranteed [Note: they meant without an individual guarantee] children, until those already here have been placed. I regret that it is no use to continue to ask for more help than we are giving, because it is not in our power to grant it.'[12] Selecting the children who would become the successful applicants was difficult. There were competing demands that had to be negotiated. There is evidence that Continental organizers, certainly in the early months of the Kindertransport, tried to prioritize the most urgent applications, which included older boys who were in danger of getting arrested and put into camps, and those who had lost one or both of their parents, as well as those who were living in children's homes.

The RCM was keen only to admit children who were easy to care for and would make a good impression on their hosts, and who were destined to be an asset to the UK. The administrative head of the RCM was Lola Hahn-Warburg, who was assisted by Grete Exiner.[13] Correspondence shows that both women felt that they had the responsibility to select those applicants who were most likely to thrive in the UK, rather than choose the potential candidates according to the urgency of their need to escape persecution. They tried to select 'high-quality' children who would be easy to place, make a good impression on the host community, and potentially make a good contribution to the economy and society in due course. In fact, some of the terminology used in the letters written by Hahn-Warburg and Exiner on behalf of the RCM was not dissimilar from the eugenicist terminology used by the Nazis. One applicant, for example, a girl called Kitty Milch, was described as 'an intelligent looking and not particularly Jewish' girl, and an example of the type of child who should be given sanctuary in the UK.[14] This was especially problematic as, by 1938, many children had lived under considerable stress. Behavioural problems were clearly an understandable reaction from children living in a very adverse environment, but they were seen as a problem that would mean that a child would not be accepted by the London RCM. Even minor problems such as bed-wetting were seen as a reason to reject an application. If the reports on the applicants suggested any additional needs, the applications had little chance of success.

Hahn-Warburg and Exiner both stated in correspondence that they had to promise the Home Office to take on only physically and mentally healthy children. Hahn-Warburg insisted that 'we have given the Home Office an undertaking that the Movement will only bring children who are 100% mentally and physically fit'.[15] Exiner wrote on 10 March 1939: 'We cannot bring mentally retarded children under any circumstances to England, even when they attend a normal school.'[16] Therefore, they rejected applications if the report on the children compiled by the Continental organizations mentioned any illnesses or additional needs. For example, the application from a boy called Hans Lang was rejected as he was described as 'a little backward in his mental development' in the report.[17] The application from a girl called Gerda Kral was also rejected: in August 1939, Exiner commented on her case and stated again that they could only take children 'who were 100% normal'. Gerda was later deported to Riga on 6 February 1942. In the case of another applicant, it was not the child herself who had been diagnosed with any illness or lived with a disability. Herta Baumfeld's mother was in a psychiatric institution, which meant that Herta's application was sent back despite the fact that the IKG had stated that the girl herself was 'completely normal'.[18] Herta was killed at Maly Trostenets on 18 September 1942.

No documentation from the Home Office with specific requirements in relation to the health status of the potential Kindertransport refugees has yet come to light. However, ideologies of eugenics were popular in the UK across the political spectrum from the early twentieth century. There were fears that the 'health of the nation' was declining, and that measures were needed to stop this development. With a better understanding of genetics, many argued in the 1920s that those with better genes should be encouraged to have children, and others should be discouraged. This might well have influenced many decision-makers regarding immigration of adults and children.

It is clear from the debates in the House of Commons that the usefulness of the children to the UK had been an important consideration when deciding on refugee policy. Furthermore, the reliance on volunteers and the lack of government funding created a pressurized environment. Even if the government did not make precise stipulations or issue any selection criteria to the organizing bodies, the RCM felt under pressure from the Home Office as they had the power to issue new rules and regulations. This the Home Office did more than once. As mentioned, in early 1939, for example, the rules regarding the exact formalities for the guarantee were changed. For the RCM, this must have added to the pressure to only admit children who would make a good impression, in order to encourage the continued offers of charitable donations and hospitality from private UK citizens that were necessary for the scheme to continue.

Another predicament related to finding foster placements. Male teenagers who were considered a priority for leaving Germany and Austria were, unsurprisingly, difficult to place with foster families. It seems that potential guarantors and foster parents in the UK were most keen to support or foster younger girls, which was not the largest group of child refugees who had applied for the scheme. The offer of hospitality for girls in that younger age group was communicated to the Continental organizing bodies. In response to this, the German organization dealing with so-called 'non-Aryan Christian' children sent a statistical analysis of the 469 applications they had received to date. This particular organization dealt with fewer children than the Jewish organizations, but there is no reason to believe that the age and gender distribution would have been very different from those of the other organizations. It is obvious that most parents were more likely to put in an application for an older child who would be considered better placed to cope with the situation of fleeing to a foreign country than a very young child. In the age group up to 6 years, 9 applications had been received for boys and 8 for girls. In the age group between 6 and 8, 16 applications had been received for boys and 4 for girls. In contrast, in the age group for 12- to 14-year-olds, 63 applications had been received for boys and 56 for girls, and in the oldest group, of those over 16 years of age, 69 applications had been received for boys and 33 for girls.[19] (The gender disparity in the last set of figures is probably due to the fact that boys over 16 years of age were in a particularly dangerous situation, while girls over the age of 16 also had the opportunity of entering the UK as a domestic servant.) The list of applicants broken down by gender and age was sent to the UK with a letter from the organizers on the Continental side that states:

> I believe this statistical analysis is quite informative in several directions. Above all one can see from it that the offered assistance to place small girls is not particularly useful to us. . . . On the contrary, we are already unable to satisfy the demand for such children. Of real benefit would be assistance regarding the older years, and especially regarding boys.[20]

This shows that the decision-making process was influenced by the preference of foster carers as well as a perceived need to admit only 'high-quality' children to the UK. Some foster parents were motivated by an image of the small innocent girl refugee who they felt would be easy to care for and integrate into their existing family structure. Some Kindertransport refugees remember that their carer wanted to show them off to their friends and the local community, and that there was an emphasis on being perceived as small, vulnerable and innocent. Marion Charles's foster mother's first remark upon meeting her concerned her height, and she showed evident displeasure that Charles did not look like a small girl (Charles was a tall 12-year-old). She then dressed up Charles in clothes that were too small to make her look more impoverished in order to gain admiration from her community for saving such a 'poor refugee girl'. This shows that some foster carers and guarantors wanted to be seen as 'saviours' and receive applause for their actions. There was also a narrative which sought to divide refugees into the good and innocent (such as vulnerable small children) and the less good, and perhaps even deserving of some negative treatment (such as young male refugees who were considered a possible security threat).

There were exceptions to these general principles: while it was very difficult for children with additional needs to escape via the Kindertransport scheme, a small number of exceptions have come to light. However, the stories told below also reveal that these children did not have much ongoing support, and that their lives after arrival in the UK were very difficult at times.

The experience of Hans Albrecht shows that it was possible for a child with additional needs to be placed on a
Kindertransport when a local refugee committee managed
to organize both financial support for his maintenance, the
guarantee and a placement for a specific individual child. Hans
Albrecht was an Austrian Jewish boy from a village called
Kleinmünchen outside Linz. He had learning difficulties and
autism. Hans remembered anti-Semitism when he was only
7 years old, and that he was not allowed to walk on his own in
the street. His place on the Kindertransport was organized via
the Worthing Refugee Committee, which had already helped
some friends of his family. Once the friends were in the UK,
Hans's escape was organized. He arrived on 15 May 1939 and
was taken in by a woman in Brighton whom he later described
as 'not nice'. He was then placed in a home for refugee children
that was led by Dr Lisa Gellner, a doctor and fellow refugee who
specialized in neurology and children with learning difficulties.
On 1 August 1939, Hans moved to Worthing with his aunt
and uncle, then he moved first to Llandudno in north Wales,
before relocating again to a village near Penrith. The changes
were very unsettling for him. On 14 April 1940, he was united
with his mother who had also managed to escape. Eventually,
in 1944, aged 13, he joined Stoately Rough, a residential school
for refugee children founded by Dr Hilde Lion, a well-known
education reformer who set up a boarding school for refugees,
one of a number of such establishments. Dr Lion described
Hans as a very kind-hearted but not very academic boy. For all
his life, Hans remembered names and dates regarding his early
life with remarkable accuracy. He said that he got on 'very well
with my memory but bad with my brain'. It is clear that Hans's
escape is a lucky exception. A 'direct' guarantee was put up by
or via the Worthing Refugee Committee, which meant that it
was only valid for Hans, and the refugee friends of the family
who were already in Worthing managed to aid the process
of getting him on a Kindertransport. Having a direct sponsor

gave children priority, but correspondence shows that many
guarantors and parents were not happy with the fact that it still
took some time for the applicant to be placed on a transport.
This policy was also not consistently applied – there were cases
when applicants were rejected even though they had a direct
individual guarantee and had a firm arrangement for a foster
placement.[21]

In Hans Albrecht's case, being united with first his aunt
and uncle and then with his mother clearly made his adjustment to life in the UK easier, despite his leaning difficulties
and autism. The few other children with additional needs that
managed to escape via the Kindertransport scheme had an
extremely difficult time understanding what was happening to
them, and struggled to adjust to life in the UK and to these –
for them – incomprehensible changes. Anne Marschner (later
Anne Senchal) and her brother Horst were two deaf children
who had attended the Jewish School for the Deaf and Dumb
– as it was called then – in the Weissensee district on the
eastern fringe of Berlin. They came from a very impoverished
Jewish family: their father had been a coal man but had left the
family, and their mother was a sewing machinist who worked
at home. They had one hearing brother called Karl Heinz. The
family lived in one room, and Anne had to share a bed with her
mother; her two brothers shared the other bed. Their experience of both their time in Germany and their time in the UK
was marred by communication difficulties. Education for deaf
children was not as advanced as it is today, and there was no
assistive technology: their mother did not really know how to
sign, and they were unable to understand much of what was
going on. Anne recalls not really understanding that she was
Jewish, or what it meant to be Jewish, as a young child.

This changed when she started attending a specialist school.
The Jewish School for the Deaf was located next to the syna-
gogue and, therefore, very visible and vulnerable to attack. In
April 1938, a group of pupils hanging out in the field behind

the school were attacked by some Hitler Youth and beaten up. Soon afterwards, during a school assembly, the headmaster, Dr Felix Reich, was arrested by eight Nazis, beaten and dragged out of the school. This was the end of lessons in the school for some months, until Reich returned in May 1939. In July 1939, he took ten of the children, including Anne and Horst, on a Kindertransport to the UK.

Anne was 10 years old at the time and remembered the large number of children at the station in Berlin before their departure. She had never been on a train before, but she was reassured by her mother who said to her 'I will be seeing you in two weeks' time.' This was affirmed by the headmaster, who reassured the children that 'they will see mum and dad again soon'. The headmaster of the Jewish Residential School for the Deaf in Nightingale Lane in Clapham, London, collected the children, and Anne remembered that Reich was arrested. Whether there was something wrong with his paperwork, or there was another reason, we do not know. Anne remembered struggling with the food they were served at the school, which consisted of a lot of white bread and tea, neither of which she had ever had before. Of course, all the other children at the school used British Sign Language, which the German children did not know. The hearing people spoke English, which they did not know either, and they were unable to lip-read English. At the school, despite being over 10 years old, Anne and three others were sent to the nursery class. Anne recalled that they did not get on well, and that they did not learn much. When the Second World War started, she did not know what was happening. This was a pattern throughout her early life: Anne's additional needs were often not met or accommodated, and she missed a lot of news and developments which other hearing people were able to catch up on more easily.

In November 1939, the German children were sent to a school in Brighton, where there were also non-Jewish deaf children. In retrospect, Anne believed that they did not have a proper education there either: they learnt some Hebrew and had some English classes, but her literacy was very poor until well into adulthood. Anne remembered getting a letter from her mother, but some parts had been cut out by the censor. She received a second, final letter in 1942. She was not particularly upset when communication eventually ceased completely, as she had not had a meaningful relationship with her mother for so long. Anne later described the condition of their relationship as being 'estranged'. The fact that other children at her school received visitors reminded her that her situation was different: 'Every three months the parents would come to visit, and I used to feel very isolated, and did not understand why my mother did not come, as she had said she would see me in two weeks' time.'

The group of children was evacuated to Wiltshire, and eventually both Anne and her brother were asked to leave the school as soon as they were 16. Anne's life as a young person was marred by not being able to get information because of her deafness and her illiteracy. From age 16 to 18, Anne lived in a hostel in Manchester with both non-Jews and hearing people; there, she trained as a dressmaker. She had very little money, hardly any clothes and little food. In fact, she became emaciated and suffered from various illnesses due to malnutrition. Again, she felt isolated. She remembered that she was taken to street celebrations when the war ended, but did not even know why people were celebrating.

Her brother in the meantime also had had a very difficult time. Looking at his life with today's knowledge of children with additional needs, we might say that, as well as being deaf, he had behavioural problems. This started at school in Berlin and continued at school in the UK. He was always in trouble, and Anne recalled that he was put in a kind of solitary confinement as punishment, and that she was told not to communicate with him either – a rule she broke. Very little was explained to either Anne or Horst, and when he left the school at 16, Anne was not told what he was going to do next. Following the end of the war, Anne finally saw him again but after two weeks he suddenly vanished. This was because he had been deported to Germany. Horst had stolen bicycles, and had been caught, arrested, convicted and deported. Years later, it was established that due judicial process had not been followed but, by then, he had re-established a life in Germany.

Anne moved from Manchester to London, but her situation did not improve much. She found out that neither of her parents was alive. Her father had died in Bergen-Belsen and her mother was murdered in a gas chamber on 28 March 1945 in Lodz. While in London, she became very depressed and tried to take her own life twice. One day, Anne had gone to the cinema and seen a Pathé news reel which showed emaciated concentration camp victims: 'That is when the reality dawned on me.' She realized what had happened to her parents and many others. Anne had no one she could talk to or who would help her to cope with this: 'I didn't tell anyone anything.'

It is remarkable that Anne managed to carry on. She eventually made some friends at the Deaf Club in London, and met her husband Stanley, also a deaf person. The couple married and had two daughters: one deaf daughter, Lana, and one hearing daughter, Gloria. The latter works as a sign language interpreter. Anne managed to claim successfully a compensation payment from the government of the Federal Republic of Germany. Most children who fled on a Kindertransport were only much later offered compensation, in 2019, and then the amount was only 2,500 Euros. When Anne visited the building that had accommodated her old school in Berlin-Weissensee, she noted a plaque commemorating the 151 deaf children from the school who had been murdered in the Holocaust.

What was common to all Kindertransport refugees was the fact that they had to part from their parents and family, and that they arrived in an unfamiliar environment. The actual journey from the Continent to the UK is remembered by some Kindertransport refugees, whereas others have little recollection of what happened. Successful applicants to the Kindertransport scheme were notified by the respective organizing bodies of their departure date. They were allowed to take two pieces of luggage: one large and a smaller one. They had to be of a size and weight that the children would be able to carry them themselves, though clearly an exemption was made from that rule for babies and toddlers. The Nazi government rules stipulated that no valuables were to be taken out of the German Reich and only a small sum of money. Many of the older children remembered the anxiety they felt because their parents had hidden a piece of jewellery or another small valuable object somewhere on their person or in their clothing. Clearly, the Continental parents did not want to let their children flee abroad completely penniless, and gave them something of value to take with them, if they could. Of course, the children also had food for the journey. Most Kindertransport refugees travelled by train.

Unsurprisingly, the moment of parting is something many remember clearly. In most cases, restrictions were imposed on how many people could bid the child farewell and where they had to say goodbye. Often only one parent could accompany the child to the station, and in many cases parents were not allowed to accompany them to the train or onto the platform. The Nazi government was happy to persecute and exclude Jews wherever they could, and they were quite happy to get rid of the Jewish children by letting them flee abroad. However, as ever, they did fear that the non-Jewish German population might object to their policies if they witnessed emotional tearful farewells at German train stations. This meant that many last moments had to take place in waiting rooms or other enclosed locations away from the platform or any public space. Many trains also left during the night, making the departure less visible to most of the general public, but this schedule was also determined by the timing of morning ferry crossings.

Trains left from the main stations of different cities such as Frankfurt and Berlin and Vienna, and later also from Prague station. The most common route was via the Hook of Holland, then onto a ferry to the port of Harwich in Essex, and often the final destination was Liverpool Street Station in London. All these places are marked with Kindertransport memorials today. Of course, if children lived away from the main departure points on the Continent, they had to travel to join a transport there, and if their placement was outside London or the southeast of England, they had to undertake further travel in the UK.

There were a number of other routes and, in some cases, children travelled by ship and even plane. In January 1939, William Dieneman and Ursula Dienemann travelled by train from Berlin to Hamburg, and then by ship, in their case on the SS *Manhattan*, to Southampton. William later remembered that he enjoyed the journey because he was given ice cream on the ship, but Ursula did not as she was feeling seasick. The journey was obviously much longer from Prague, and some children travelled by air. There is a well-known photo of a small child in the arms of Nicholas Winton, one of the organizers of the Kindertransport from Prague, on the steps to a plane.

The transports were usually accompanied by a small number of adults, who in some cases were social workers and teachers, and these adults acted as guardians for the journey, but they had to return to the Continent shortly after arriving. The child-to-adult ratio was large and many of the older child refugees were given the responsibility for small children on the trains and ferries, a task that some cherished and others resented. Harry Weinberger recalled in an interview that his sister had a place on a Kindertransport from Prague and that he was persuaded by an acquaintance that he should accompany the transport and then just stay in the UK.[22] Weinberger was 15 years old at the time and was apparently given an arm-band marking him out as an accompanying adult. He had grandparents in the

UK, which might explain how this actually worked out. There are no other records of accompanying adults not returning to Germany.

Files show that, at times, there was frantic correspondence between the Continental organizing committees and helpers in the Netherlands, who would usually provide some food and drink to the children, when it had been noticed along the way that some necessary document was still missing. This might also have been an opportunity to get Harry Weinberger some ad hoc documents, and thus to facilitate his admission to the UK.

The individual transports ranged in size from very large (such as the first transport from Vienna with 400 child refugees on 10 December 1938) to quite small (such as the last transport from Vienna in August 1939, which consisted of only 35 child refugees). The last Kindertransport from Prague was already assembled on 1 September 1939, when the outbreak of the Second World War prevented it from leaving. Many of the children who were supposed to escape on that transport were later murdered in the Holocaust.

5

Placements

Upon arrival in the UK, some of the children were found temporary placements in camps and children's homes such as Dovercourt Camp – a holiday camp near Harwich which was empty in the winter months – or Pakefield Camp near Lowestoft. These were mainly for slightly older children; younger children were accommodated in a children's home in Broadstairs, Kent. All of these were in use in the early months of the Kindertransport. East Anglian holiday camps proved somewhat unsuitable in the winter, and the supervision and selection practices left something to be desired. Some child refugees would later describe how potential foster parents visited at weekends to pick a child they wished to look after. Some children felt that this created a 'cattle market' atmosphere. They recalled that the potential parents preferred smaller, prettier children and that no attempt was made to match up foster parents according to the background and needs of the child.

Other Kindertransport refugees were transferred straight onto trains to London, either arriving at London Liverpool Street Station, if they had arrived at Harwich, or Waterloo Station, if they had travelled via Southampton. They were then accommodated either in communal settings or with individual foster families. The first call for foster parents put out by public appeal in Britain elicited 500 immediate responses from those willing to accommodate children. There is little evidence that the number of Kindertransportees was ever limited by a lack of foster parents during the ten-month duration of the scheme, which is astonishing. From both the memoirs and interviews of child refugees and reports by the RCM, it seems that foster placements were offered by people from all backgrounds, social classes and income brackets. Those who could not manage to afford the maintenance of the child were given a payment by the RCM, although the organization obviously preferred it if the cost was met by the guarantor or the foster family. For very young children, there were no alternatives to placements in foster families, and ideally the placements for those below primary school age were found before they arrived. Many teenagers preferred communal settings where they did not have to adapt to the very specific, personalized rules of a family – which would undoubtedly in most cases be very different from those of their birth family – and where they could live more independently and with other young people who had had similar experiences.[1]

While there were appeals for both financial support and offers of placements on a national level, such as from the Lord Baldwin Fund, the majority of fostering arrangements had to be organized at the local level. This was often done via the local Refugee Committees, which existed in many areas but had hitherto mainly dealt with adults or whole families. On 12 December 1938, Eva Hartree, chair of the children's subcommittee of the Cambridge Refugee Committee, published an appeal in a local newspaper, the *Cambridge Daily News*, asking for people who would be willing to offer homes:

> We would greatly welcome offers to take one or more children for what, we hope, will be a limited time, until other arrangements can be made for their parents to rejoin them, within

Great Britain or elsewhere. Most of the children are of Jewish race, but there are also a great number of 'non-Aryan' Christians among them, and these, as the Archbishop of Canterbury has said, are a special responsibility of the Christian Community. There are also orphans . . . and it may be that some may wish to take a child more permanently. We should be especially pleased to receive such offers. . . . All offers of homes should be sent to Mrs Hutton, 1 Chaucer Road, who will send a form to be filled by the applicant in order that all particulars may be registered.[2]

This letter did not give an accurate impression of the actual situation, unfortunately. Firstly, it was very difficult for the Kindertransport refugees' parents to join them in Britain or find refuge elsewhere. By writing this letter in this way, Hartree might have inadvertently created an expectation that the arrangement would be quite short-term. Secondly, although Hartree mentioned that most of the children were Jewish, she did mention the possibility of providing a temporary home to a Christian child, and this might have given the impression that the balance between Jewish and Christian children was more equal (in reality, only about 20 per cent of the Kindertransport refugees who found sanctuary in the UK came from families who defined themselves as Christian). Thirdly, the letter mentions the possibility of taking in an orphan child and implies that adoption might be a possibility. The letter refers to the fact that many of the child refugees arriving on the first transport were from an orphanage in Berlin. However, although they lived there (some only for a short time), this did not necessarily mean that they had no parents. Some lived in the children's home only because their persecuted parents were unable to support them and thought they would be safer there than at home.

The family of Ruth Auerbach (later Ruth Schwiening) was originally from Wroclaw, but they moved to Berlin after her father was arrested by the Nazis. There, her mother put 3-year-old Ruth and her slightly older brother in the Jewish children's home while she was trying to find emigration possibilities for all the family. Ruth Schwiening was chosen for a Kindertransport ahead of her brother as it was believed it was easier to find a foster placement for a girl.[3] In this way, she left the orphanage and arrived on the first transport in London on 2 December 1938. However, she had a sibling and parents, despite coming from an orphanage. The aforementioned appeal in the newspaper also implied that there were no specific requirements for the foster parents and that it was purely a matter of registering. This was not the case as there were checks regarding the suitability of foster placements. The letter was aimed to elicit a positive response from the broadest range of people, and the most offers of assistance, but it was ultimately giving inaccurate information and the wrong impression.

There was an element of good fortune as to whether the foster placements for the Kindertransport refugees were able to nurture the child successfully or whether they failed on various fronts and caused further trauma. The 3-year-old twins Lotte and Susi Bechhöfer were failed by their foster parents. The couple decided to hide the fact that they were not their biological children in public, and this was interrelated with other extremely damaging behaviour from the foster parents, especially the foster father. The twins' birth parents were Rosa Bechhöfer, a 37-year-old Jewish woman, and Otto Hald, who was 28 and considered Aryan. Almost from the start, their relationship was considered illegal as the Nuremberg Laws were in the process of being passed, forbidding sexual relationships between Jews and non-Jews. They were not married when Rosa gave birth to the twins Lotte and Susi on 17 May 1936 in the Jewish maternity hospital in Munich. Otto did not dare visit, and it became clear that Rosa would have to bring up the children without the support of a father. As most of Rosa's family were not particularly supportive, she placed the twins in the Antonienheim, a Jewish orphanage in Munich, and started working as a cook and housekeeper for several Jewish families in the city. Rosa visited the twins on her free Sundays. Social worker Alice Bendix was the director of the orphanage. An energetic and well-organized woman, she tried to find a safe place abroad for the twins. Initially, Rosa was completely taken aback by the suggestion that her children should be sent abroad. She did not want to give up them up, even though she could not care for them full-time. However, before long, Rosa realized that it was too dangerous for her children to stay in Germany, and she consented to them leaving Munich on a Kindertransport to the UK.

Because they were so young, a foster placement for the twins was arranged in advance of their departure. Fred Legge, a Baptist minister from Cardiff, and his wife Audrey had agreed to provide a home for Lotte and Susi Bechhöfer. The Legges had not been able to have biological children, and this was something that Fred especially found very difficult to live with. Upon arrival in the family, the Legges changed the girls' names immediately from Lotte and Susi to Eunice Mary and Grace Elizabeth Legge, respectively. Fred tried to pretend that the twins were his birth children and got very annoyed if anyone asked about their origin, despite the fact that members of the local community knew how they came to live with the Legges.

By the time the twins started at a local primary school, the Second World War was dominating most people's thoughts and the girls were teased for being German. This upset Fred greatly – mainly because he wanted the children to be seen as his own, but also because he did not want them to be reminded of their past. He immediately removed Susi and Lotte from the local school and sent them instead to a small private school in Llandaff called Elm Tree House.

Tragically, Lotte became very unwell when she was 7. She fell behind with her schoolwork, started walking in an unusual way, and her character appeared to change. After numerous hospital visits, Lotte was diagnosed with a brain tumour. The tumour was removed surgically, but from then on until her death, aged 35, Lotte needed constant care. This whole traumatic experience affected Susi negatively as well. Fred was still unable to acknowledge the twins' origins and he used to tell Susi, 'You are Grace Elizabeth Legge, and you are mine.' At some point, Susi (Grace) was sent to boarding school, which was a relief to her. She enjoyed her time there and preferred it to living with her foster parents.

Only years later was Susi able to speak fully about what happened during her childhood. Fred Legge was not only very controlling, he also sexually abused his foster daughter. When Susi was back from boarding school, she would have to spend hours locked away with Fred in his study, where he would abuse her, and the same would happen in her bedroom at night. She felt that Fred had complete control over her life, and she only managed to survive the repeated trauma by dissociating herself from these events.

These traumatic memories had a life-long detrimental effect on her mental health. Susi led an outwardly successful life – as an adult, she trained as a nurse, found a partner, got married, and the couple had a son. She only found out about the circumstances of her arrival in Britain when she heard a radio programme in which the Kindertransport was discussed. Subsequently, Susi spent years researching her past and eventually discovered that her mother had been deported to Auschwitz and murdered there in 1943. She also found out that she had surviving relatives in the USA, and even met a half-sister on her biological father's side. Her story attracted public attention: she co-wrote a memoir together with Jeremy Jacobs, was featured in a TV documentary and became the basis for a character in the novel *Austerlitz* by the writer W. G. Sebald.[4] Susi was not very happy about either the memoir or the documentary, and certainly not about her story being used in the novel without any acknowledgement of its origin.

Susi's Kindertransport story is undoubtedly one of the most traumatic ones. There are complicated reasons for this trauma, which lie both in the Nazi persecution and the murder of Susi's family, and in the UK government's decision only to admit minors under this scheme. In this case, the trauma was further compounded by the criminal and abusive behaviour of her foster father. The way that foster placements were approved and allocated was not in accordance with established criteria, nor was the process overseen by trained professionals. There was little guidance on how foster carers were to deal with the children's connection to their birth family. Susi died in 2018 but published another autobiographically inspired text with the title *Rosa* prior to her death.[5]

The body of testimony from the foster parents is not large. There are letters between foster parents and birth parents, but these often follow the polite conventions expected of such exchanges, with the birth parents expressing gratitude and the foster parents expressing sympathy, as is the case with the letters between Milena Roth's birth mother and foster mother. Ilse Majer's foster placement was with Lady Howard Stepney who wrote very positively about her charge to her birth parents: 'your daughter is *very* charming and we are delighted with her'.[6]

It is difficult to discern a comprehensive picture of everyday life in a family in which a Kindertransport refugee found a foster placement. A very small number of memoirs, including some by former foster siblings, outline the challenges of living with a newly arrived child refugee. Ann Chadwick's family gave a home to a 5-year-old girl named Suzie in 1939. Ann herself was of the same age at the time. Chadwick draws on some essays her mother wrote, for a course of training to work with children with behavioural needs, to examine the difficulties due to the changed family dynamic. In these texts, Ann's mother points out that it was the birth daughter, Ann, who started to display challenging behaviour after the arrival of the Kindertransport refugee, Suzie:

[My mother] highlights it was me rather than Suzie who was traumatized by our coming together and that once I recommenced bed-wetting and exhibited jealous tantrums and withdrawal symptoms, she had to resort to help from the Child Guidance Clinic to help me readjust. . . . It is not surprising. Both of us had been only children, adored and spoilt by our respective parents . . . We did fight too.[7]

Clearly, this particular foster family had the insight and resources to help both children adjust to their new situation. Not all foster parents were able to do this and thus many placements broke down, and Kindertransport refugees had to change placements frequently.

Other placements in foster families were very successful. Renate Kress (later Renate Collins) was 5 years old when she escaped Prague on a Kindertransport. Like the Bechhöfer twins, she was also placed with a Baptist minister and his wife in south Wales. However, while Sidney and Arianwen Coplestone were very supportive of Renate's new life in their community in Porth, they also did everything to encourage her connection to her Jewish faith and helped her remember her birth parents. Renate's birth parents had exchanged letters and photographs with Renate's foster parents before her arrival. Renate attended church with her foster parents, but her foster father always taught her about her Jewish background and, as an adult, Renate defined herself as a Jew. Renate lost her parents and sixty-two other members of her family in the Holocaust. In 1947, after learning of Renate's parents' deaths, Sidney and Arianwen adopted Renate, who was then 14 years old. By then, she had spent nine years in Porth.

Renate did not know who had brought her over to the UK and how the Kindertransport had worked; neither did her adoptive father fully understand. It is not true that no efforts were made to check on foster placements and to find out about the progress of the Kindertransport refugees. However, often the child refugees would not remember anyone ever visiting the family. It is also true that the approach of the 'visitors' on behalf of the RCM was not child-centred. This was undoubtedly partially related to the need to rely on volunteers because of the lack of government financial and organizational support.

Although the central committee of the RCM made the decision about suitable children for the Kindertransports, it soon became clear that once the children needed to be placed and the placements needed to be checked out, and eventually the children 'visited', the organization needed to have local committees. Committees were set up in twelve areas of the UK, corresponding to the Regional Defence Areas.[8] Each region had a number of regional committees: for example, Cardiff was supposed to have four, Birmingham eighteen and Oxford twenty. These local committees were 'to undertake visiting work'. Most were only set up after the outbreak of war, which meant that the initial allocation happened without much effort at all to match the child refugee with an appropriate placement.

However, it is not correct to conclude that no efforts were made to provide the best possible solution under difficult circumstances over the next years. Records show that there was extensive correspondence between potential foster carers and the RCM and the local committee, and between actual foster families and the committees as well. There are numerous files that show that some families were visited, and some assessment of the situation was taking place. However, the records also show that some of the social care visitors lacked training, and in some cases the focus was clearly more on the needs of the foster parents than of the children.

Ruth Simmons was one such social care visitor. She worked in Region 9, which included a large area and the counties of Shropshire, Staffordshire, Herefordshire, Worcestershire and Warwickshire. In Warwickshire, there were between 100 and 250 Kindertransport refugees in 1939, which gives an indication that the overall number of placements in this particular region must have been large.

Simmons came from a successful middle-class family that was committed to helping refugees. Simmons's father had a jewellery business in Birmingham, and her mother was originally from Frankfurt. From 1933 onwards, they tried to help Jewish refugees who had to flee to the UK. In 1938, Ruth Simmons initially went to Paris to establish her own fashion studio, but then returned to Birmingham after learning about the November Pogroms. Young, energetic and committed to her work, she was clearly motivated to assist refugees, but some of her comments over the years show the prejudices of her class and background and her lack of training. This becomes clear from reading the files on one particular offer of a foster placement. She was sent to assess this offer of a placement for one or two girls aged between 9 and 11 which had reached the RCM in 1941. Simmons assessed the home of Mr and Mrs Phillips and made notes to be able to file a report. We can read that the 'home is excellent, small but very well off, clean and quiet'. The next line describes the potential foster parents: 'Mr Phillips is a civil servant. They have no children of their own and want a companion for Mrs Phillips.'[9] This latter expression, of course, would set alarm bells ringing in modern ears: fostering a child should not be motivated by the need to alleviate an adult's lack of companionship. Furthermore, we learn from the file that the Phillipses were looking to foster a well-bred child who 'would fit in with our lives', and that they wanted to offer a placement to one or two 'really attractive girls'.[10] While the sexual undertone that we might read into this description is probably misplaced, it is still clear that such an assessment of the suitability of a foster placement is inadequate.

By 1941, two years after the Kindertransport refugees began arriving in the UK, the RCM had managed to develop a questionnaire with more probing and useful questions. However, as many Kindertransport refugees had to change foster families once or more, the questionnaire had its uses to determine further suitable foster families. It included questions regarding the religious convictions and attitudes to religious education of the potential foster parents, possible knowledge of the German language and a question enquiring whether the foster parents were aware that the child refugee was not an orphan. Ruth Simmons's assessment does not seem to have asked about these important points. This shows that the way many of the well-meaning but underqualified volunteers carried out this vital work potentially lacked rigour and was not centred on the needs of the child.

The question of religion was obviously an important one. It was clear from the beginning that the scheme would not be able to offer all Jewish children a Jewish foster placement, and there was definitely little chance that the child refugees would only be placed with a family which belonged to the same branch of Judaism – i.e. that Orthodox children would only be placed in Orthodox homes, and children from Liberal Jewish homes would find themselves only in a closely matching foster placement. Firstly, there were too many different possibilities, and secondly, the definition of some branches of Judaism varied between Germany and the UK. However, the overriding point is the fact that, as there were only around 300,000 Jewish people in the UK in 1933, it was unlikely that enough Jewish foster homes could be found for the Jewish children.

As discussed, the parents knew this and many consented to their children being placed in a non-Jewish home. Of course, many of these parents were hoping to be reunited with their children much quicker than was the case (if they were reunited at all). However, living in a non-Orthodox environment was not really possible for Orthodox children. A group of Orthodox boys who were housed in Dovercourt Camp after their arrival in December 1938 wrote an angry letter to the Chief Rabbi, complaining about the lack of kosher food in the camp. The Chief Rabbi's representative, Rabbi Dr Solomon Schonfeld, acted immediately and managed to organize food that was prepared according to the Jewish dietary laws. Schonfeld played an active part in rescuing Orthodox child refugees, as well as in the heated debates that raged within the Jewish communities. These debates were public and even reported on in the *Jewish Chronicle*. In December 1938, the newspaper wrote: 'Already one hears of a struggle between Zionists and non-Zionists, between Orthodox and non-Orthodox, between the charity-contributors and social workers, between all the different factions of Anglo-Jewry It is surely necessary to place the future well-being and happiness of these refugee children before all private prejudices and vested interests.'[11]

Schonfeld consequently set out to organize transports that would be specifically tailored for Orthodox children. He placed most of the 300 children he brought to the UK in two Orthodox schools that he was in charge of. He even accommodated some in his own home. Some of Schonfeld's actions were controversial and were criticized by other Kindertransport organizers. For example, Schonfeld was against letting Kindertransport trains travel on the Sabbath, and some argued that he was endangering the lives of the children as they needed to leave the German Reich as quickly as possible.[12]

As mentioned, Zionist organizations also used the Kindertransport scheme to get persecuted Jewish minors out of harm's way and to the UK. The aim of most of these organizations was for young Jews to make Aliyah – that is, to emigrate to Palestine and help with the setting up of Eretz Israel, the Jewish homeland. Palestine at the time was under British Mandate, and the British administration was trying to calm tensions with the local Arab population by restricting immigration to an absolute minimum. Some Zionist organizations decided that immigration to the UK was the next best thing, and were hoping that the young people could be trained in a trade or agriculture in the UK, which would be useful once they eventually emigrated from the UK to Palestine.

Gwrych Castle, near Abergele
With permission from Andrea Hammel

Arieh Handler was a young Zionist activist and organizer. He was born in 1915 in Bohemia into a Jewish family, but later lived in Germany. He finished school in 1933 and was very active in the religious Zionist Youth movement, similar to B'nei Akiva in the UK. Despite his young age, he travelled around Europe (with special permission of the Nazi government) to find placements for young Jews outside Germany, to prepare them for emigrating to Palestine. He found it very difficult to please anyone in the UK because of the strict immigration rules. Only once the Kindertransport scheme came into being was he able to get larger numbers of young people who had signed up to the Zionist cause into the country. He was then instrumental in setting up agricultural training camps (*Hachsharot*) in the UK. The largest of them was Gwrych Castle, near Abergele in north Wales.[13] Handler was very critical of the idea of the Kindertransport: he used the scheme as a means to an end – namely, to get young people away from

Nazi persecution and into training for emigration. Handler was against the idea of Jewish refugees being placed in non-Jewish homes and he would later argue that this was the reason why a large number of former Kindertransport refugees left 'the Jewish fold':

> And they were placed in non-Jewish places, not in *Hachsharot*, and I wanted them to be in *Hachsharot*, . . . we wanted them to remain together. And we kept those together as much as possible. But the remainder, those who were sent into non-Jewish homes, very nice of those British people who took them on. . . . Out of the 10,000 Kindertransport people a maximum of 3000 or 4000 remained in the Jewish fold.[14]

Handler later described arguing with one of the prominent administrators at Bloomsbury House, the headquarters of many refugee organizations, who felt that the most important aim was simply to get as many children as possible away from National Socialist persecution and save their lives. Finding a placement that matched a child's religious affiliation was considered a secondary concern. Handler, on the other hand, felt that this was very important and that the young people should stay together and join *Hachsharot*, as, in his opinion, emigration to Palestine should be the ultimate aim. He argued that communal placements were preferable because this would prepare them for the communal life of the kibbutzim. Handler worried that living in a family as a foster child would make them less suitable for the life that he envisaged for them in the new homeland in Palestine. As he later argued in an interview:

> The main thing is to save lives. And if you have a non-Jewish family prepared to accept them, let's send them, wherever it is, they survive, and that's the most important thing, very logical. What was our argument? We said yes, if there is no other way, that is a way. But if we can find a way to place 200 boys and girls

in a Castle which was then given to me for the duration of the
war, Gwrych Castle, in North Wales, next to Abergele . . . If we
can get such a place, and we can place 200 boys and girls there,
in their surroundings, it is better than to put them to a family
which has their own problems, because there is a war on. And I
believe that we were right.[15]

The fact that many Kindertransportees did not remain 'in
the Jewish fold' is something that some religious leaders regret,
of course, as did Arieh Handler. There are no official statis-
tics, and the nature of religious observance is very difficult
to define, but Handler's estimation that, of the 10,000 child
refugees who arrived, only about 4,000 considered themselves
religious Jews by the 1980s is possibly not far off. However,
about 20 per cent of those arrivals had come from families that
did not define themselves as Jewish, but rather were externally
and newly classified as such by Nazi Race Laws. Furthermore,
the second half of the twentieth century generally saw a move
towards a more secular society; many Jews who had grown up
in religious Anglo-Jewish families married non-Jewish partners
and decided not to affiliate themselves either with Judaism
or, indeed, with any religious observance. Therefore, if around
40 per cent of those who came to the UK on a Kindertransport
remained religious Jews, we might argue that this is approxi-
mately in line with general trends and not a reflection of the
process by which they were placed with non-Jewish foster
families. However, it needs to be remembered that we are only
dealing with estimates; the information available is not sufficiently complete to make accurate statistical comparisons.

Having a preference for living in more communal settings
might be seen as surprising, but it is one that many older child
refugees expressed, regardless of whether they wanted to live
in a *Hachshara*. Study of the life stories and memoirs of the
former child refugees does suggest that many of the older children and teenagers did prefer to live in communal settings,

whether camps like Grwych Castle or hostels and boarding schools, and eventually universities. They were often happy to get away from unfamiliar family rules and traditions, and to live somewhere where they could give each other support and help each other adapt to their new lives.

Handler could only get larger numbers of refugee young-sters into the UK once the Kindertransport scheme was opened in December 1938. Before that, even if he could con-vince a farmer to take on a refugee trainee, he could not easily get such trainees a visa to come to the UK. Handler felt that, before the end of 1938, placing a teenage refugee as an agricul-tural trainee was much easier in Denmark or the Netherlands than in the UK. Once Britain was at war with Germany, the Kindertransport stopped, and it became difficult to travel at all. However, Handler did manage to bring in a small number of young refugees after September 1939 by getting them work permits for the UK. These were available because the British government realized that, as a consequence of so many able-bodied young people joining the Army and auxiliary services, there was a labour shortage in the agricultural sector.

The *Hachshara* at Gwrych Castle offered community to traumatized young people. Being part of a Zionist training camp also provided a sense of purpose, as did the involve-ment in practical work with the local community in Abergele. Handler felt that it was also important that the Jewish refugees were visible in the local area and useful to the local economy to gain acceptance and show their usefulness. In later life, Handler saw Gwrych as a successful venture and as an espe-cially important *Hachshara*, due to its size and the fact that accommodating the youngsters together kept them within a Jewish community and did not expose them to non-Jewish foster parents during the war. Besides wanting the youths to stay in a Jewish environment, Zionist leaders such as Handler also wanted them to live communally and work on the land or in related trade, all in preparation for making Aliyah. Handler was therefore looking for large properties where communal living would be possible. He was offered Gwyrch Castle, which was originally built between 1812 and 1822 by Lloyd Hesketh Bamford-Hesketh, before passing to the Dundonald family. However, by 1939, Lord Dundonald had not been using the property for over fifteen years and so he offered it for free to the Ministry of Labour and then to the British Forces. Both declined to take up the offer, but Handler accepted and took over the Castle for his *Hachshara* on 28 August 1939, to house refugee children. However, as the Castle had not been used for so long, it had fallen into disrepair. In any case, it had probably never been kitted out with certain modern conveniences, and certainly not for so many residents. Most of the new residents had come from a camp in Kent where they had had to live in tents, so many were excited by the idea of living in a castle, and saw it as an improvement on their former accommodation.

Walter Bingham, a Kindertransport refugee from Germany, later discussed his memories of being one of the first youngsters forming an advance party to Gwrych Castle from Great Engeham Farm in Kent, where he had been placed after his arrival on a Kindertransport. When Walter first caught sight of Gwrych Castle, he thought it was magnificent. He was particularly struck by the oak panelled entrance, a marble staircase, and rooms with very large open fireplaces, but reality set in very quickly. There was no electricity and inadequate toilet and bathroom facilities. The accommodation at Gwrych had been designed for an aristocratic family and a handful of servants to support them – most likely less than 15 people in all. Now Gwrych Castle was expected to accommodate 200.

This meant that the heating and the sanitary arrangements were never entirely satisfactory. The other challenge was the fact that there was very little adult supervision, and the leaders were mainly inexperienced and young. Many tasks, even the cooking, needed to be carried out by the child refugees themselves – with mixed results. Despite these challenges, there are many former Gwrych residents who remember the strong sense of community, and the fact that living with other young refugees helped them to cope with hearing about the increasingly difficult situation back on the Continent. The *Hachshara* at Gwrych Castle offered community to traumatized young people

Others voiced a less positive assessment of this particular setting. One child refugee who lived at Gwrych, Ruth Wesson, recalled that many of the teenagers fell ill, and she blamed this on the difficult sanitary and heating situation at the Castle, the inadequate food and the lack of adult supervision. She felt that schooling was virtually non-existent and that the adults who were supposed to supervise the teenagers were largely occupied with their own affairs. Unsurprisingly, some of the teenagers also fell in love with each other, and some had sexual relationships which resulted in at least one unplanned pregnancy. Probably the most tragic occurrence at the castle was the death of David Kowalski, who was only 12 years old. He had fled from the German town of Halberstadt with two others and is said to have been the youngest resident of the Gwrych *Hachshara*. When he fell seriously ill, he was moved to a hospital in Liverpool, but sadly he did not recover and died.

There were other possibilities for communal placements for older Kindertransport refugees. Some British boarding schools provided free places for refugees, some foster families put their charges into a boarding school, and there were so-called 'exile schools'. William Dieneman attended Avondale School in Bristol and recalled feeling secure and happy there, and receiving a good education. Bea Green's guarantor and foster carer also afforded her a private education. The foster mother was an older woman, and she even made provisions for Bea and another Kindertransport refugee in her will.

Being educated within the private school system certainly afforded certain privileges and many of the Kindertransport refugees who had this experience received a good education and achieved success in exams. But there were downsides to being an outsider in a very closed club as well. It seems that most of the adults in charge had little knowledge of inter-cultural communication and that often the children were left bewildered by the unfamiliar traditions. Bea Green remembered how she was made to play cricket for the first time: 'They strapped funny things to my legs and gave me a wooden thing and told me to go out to hit the ball. . . . What did it mean to be out for a duck?'[16] The term 'bewilderment' was used by others. A boy who was put in a boarding school immediately after arriving at Harwich remembered:

> I was taken apart from my brothers. I didn't know what happened to them. On the railway station at Harwich I was met by a gaunt gentleman who turned out to be a headmaster. I didn't speak English and he didn't speak German. It was all done by motion. Half an hour later I was in school, dressed in school uniform, like the other boys. Totally bewildering.[17]

How the Kindertransport refugees should be educated was another contentious issue. Most children of primary school age were simply enrolled in local primary schools. Most of these made little provision to help the child refugees learn English; the children were thrown in at the deep end. There were also incidences of bullying because of the children's origin as neither staff nor fellow pupils had been prepared for the Kindertransport refugees' arrival.

Things were more difficult for older children, or when the refugees grew older during the war years. Some of these Kindertransport refugees were very disappointed when they were not allowed to follow the educational path they had originally anticipated. They encountered prejudices that a basic education should be 'good enough' for a refugee, and that they should earn their own money as soon as possible. In part, this debate was linked to the initial idea that the Kindertransport refugees would be transmigrants who would only come to the UK temporarily to be trained as skilled workers – not professionals – and would then migrate somewhere else. The pass cards the RCM issued for each refugee read: 'This document of identity is issued with the approval of His Majesty's Government in the United Kingdom to Young Persons to be admitted to the United Kingdom for Educational Purposes under the care for the Inter-Aid committee for children.'[18]

This aspect had been discussed in the House of Commons debate, as reported earlier in the 'Escape' chapter of this book. In the debate, the point was made that the British government was willing to admit a larger number of refugees if it was only on a temporary basis, and if they would, after training in the UK, settle elsewhere, either in countries of the British Empire or in other areas. The Home Secretary Sir Samuel Hoare stated:

> We are prepared to look sympathetically and favourably upon proposals of this kind. While the absorptive powers of this country might be limited as far as permanent residents are concerned, we certainly could take in a larger number of refugees for a temporary period, provided they were eventually to be settled in some other part of the world. For instance, if we take as an example settlement in various parts of the Colonial Empire.[19]

The Annual Reports of the RCM between 1939 and 1942 repeatedly confirm this intention that the child refugees should emigrate farther, and not permanently stay in the UK, although it is not entirely clear how strictly the government would have enforced this idea that all those over 18 and who had been trained would be required to move elsewhere.

In any case, the hostilities of the Second World War prevented this policy from being carried out on a large scale. Some Kindertransport refugees migrated farther, some were interned and were then sent to Australia and Canada, but more refugees than expected had to stay in the UK because travelling abroad was extremely difficult. The RCM Annual Reports mentioned cases in which the Kindertransport refugee had migrated again frequently. It is unclear why they were so keen on this particular policy. Was it to show that the children would not permanently settle in the UK? Was the RCM worried about its financial responsibility if the children stayed?

Although, undoubtedly, the majority of the Kindertransport refugees lived in England, a smaller number were placed in Wales, Scotland and Northern Ireland. Besides the communal setting of Llandough and Gwrych Castle, there was the Czechoslovak State School in Wales, which had relocated to Llanwrted Wells. The school offered places for over 100 children, some of whom had come on a Kindertransport. Initiated by the Czechoslovak government-in-exile, it provided a communal educational experience for child refugees who had come to the UK on their own, or child refugees who had come with their parents, and to children whose parents were part of the government-in-exile and the Czechoslovak Forces. Memories of this school are overwhelmingly positive. Many Kindertransport refugees were also placed with foster families in Wales, and it seems to be the case that many of these were part of the group who had fled from Prague and thus arrived three or four months after the first trains from Germany and Austria.

Kindertransport refugees who were placed in Scotland also often lived in communal settings. The reason for this was less the concern to give the child refugees a sense of community and the ability to gain support from others with similar experience than a fear of teenage delinquency, especially in relation to boys. There was a fear that 'unattached youth' were up to no good, and that they needed to be placed in homes or hostels that provided a regimented routine and left no time for anything that could be considered irregular. This meant again that care was not tailored to the needs of the individual child refugee but to the perceived need of society.[20] In many cases, the refugees were placed in the same residential settings as non-refugees and neither the supervising adults nor the other residents were prepared and informed about the circumstances of the refugees' previous lives. Thus, these settings, despite being communal, often did not manage to engender mutual support.

In Northern Ireland, arriving Kindertransport refugees were placed together with a small number of other, older refugees at Ballyrolly House, a derelict stone farm, just 6 miles outside Mountstewart at Millisle on the Ards Peninsula, about 20 miles from Belfast.[21] The Kindertransport refugees arrived in summer 1939 and helped to transform the derelict buildings into functioning accommodation and to establish a working farm growing oats, carrots, potatoes, cabbages, cauliflower, and Brussels sprouts, as well as eventually keeping nearly 2,000 chickens, 8 cows and 2 large Clydesdale horses. The building had been leased from a local man by Barney Hurwitz, the president of the Belfast Jewish congregation. The adults established a small synagogue on the farm and the young refugees attended the local school.

Economic pressures meant that many Kindertransport refugees who had settled in Wales, Scotland and Northern Ireland moved to other parts of the UK or abroad as soon as they turned 18, or after the end of the war. Despite its Zionist aim and the community spirit, from the 1940s onwards the Gwrych Castle *Hachshara* slowly lost more and more residents. Some of the older refugees were interned, and other moved away at 18 to urban centres such as Manchester, where they found better-paid employment. Of course, not all Kindertransportees resettled in England: there were always exceptions, such as Ellen Davis who stayed all her life in the Swansea area, or Josef Kitzler, who lived on Millisle Farm and then settled in Ulster and became a successful businessman.

It is clear that the experiences of Kindertransport refugees in different placements were very varied. There were many permutations that contributed to the refugees either experiencing further trauma in inadequate settings or the feeling of being nurtured in better placements. What can be said, though, is that placements that let them stay connected in one form or another with their former lives in the originating country and helped them to find a purpose in their new host community were probably the most successful.

6

War

Some Kindertransport refugees were shocked when the Second World War broke out, although many older ones were clearly as informed of developments as their British friends or foster families.

One of the most immediate and drastic changes that was caused by the outbreak of war was the cessation of the postal service between the German Reich and the UK. While some families managed to make complicated arrangements whereby letters were sent via third countries such as Switzerland or even the USA, many children did not receive any communications from their parents or families after early September 1939. The International Red Cross later facilitated very limited communication via so-called 'Red Cross letters', which sometimes could also be sent from ghettos or camps. Renate Collins received a last communication from her mother, grandmother and uncle on the occasion of her birthday. It was dated 10 June 1942 and read: 'Many birthday wishes. We think continually of you. Are well, hope you are too. Much love, kind regards and thanks to your foster parents. Mammie, Grandmother, Felix.'[1]

Eva Mosbacher was a regular correspondent and wrote long letters focusing on both everyday life and her emotions. Her letters showed great insight and empathy with the difficult situation her parents found themselves in. Between her arrival in the UK and the end of August 1939, she wrote frequently, often asking her parents to write more often (which was unusual, as in most cases it was the parents who urged the children to write more regularly). After September 1939, Eva's letters are shorter. The first letter sent after the outbreak of the war is dated 'Cambridge, 11.9.1939', with an addition that the letter was sent via Stockholm. It is the first letter that Eva wrote in English, possibly because it was thought that otherwise her letter would not be delivered by the British Postal Service as it would not pass the scrutiny of the censor. From then on, most of her letters are much shorter than previously, but she did revert to German again. They are sent via someone in Lucerne in Switzerland, or addressed to other relatives. Besides the letters she sent via relatives, which did not always reach her parents, she sent many short telegram messages via the International Red Cross. It is clear that not all of these reached the intended party either. The parents expressed their sadness about the lack of longer correspondence. On 8 March 1940, Eva explained in a short message on a Red Cross form, 'I am not allowed to write in a different way any more – the censor has forbidden it – I have a lot of work with my exams – the grandparents are well – lots of kisses.' The last message Eva received from her parents is dated 3 May 1942: 'We are pleased that you had a good holiday. We are trying to stay healthy and brave.'[2] Six days later, her parents were deported.

The start of the war also meant that several government policies were introduced that made life for some of the recently arrived child refugees especially difficult. One such policy was the evacuation of vulnerable people out of British towns and cities. Already during the first days of September 1939, 1.5 million evacuees were sent to rural locations considered to be safer than the urban areas that they had resided in previously. Evacuation was voluntary, but many urban schools were closed and whole classes were evacuated, sometimes with their teachers. This happened to Martha Blend, who was supposed to leave London with her classmates.

Martha Blend had lived with her parents in Vienna as an only child. On 10 June 1939, aged 9, she had left them, and her familiar surroundings, on a Kindertransport. Her foster parents, whom she called aunt and uncle, were a Yiddish-speaking Jewish couple originally from Poland who lived in the East End of London. The couple were childless, and her foster mother devoted herself to Martha's care. Her foster parents did not have a lot of formal education and had a low level of literacy. Martha went to a local school until the evacuation notice reached the family, and they dutifully prepared her for her journey out of London. Martha later wrote in her memoir:

> Then came news that the scheduled evacuation of London school children would take place in two days' time. Once again my case was packed, and with my gas mask hung over my shoulder, and a label on my blazer, my aunt took me to join a crocodile of similarly equipped children in the playground of our school.

> Standing there I had a strong sense of déjà vu: Crowds of children, hand luggage, farewells – hadn't I braced myself to endure this before? I decided then and there that enough was enough. . . . I dug in my heels and said: 'I am not going.' 'But you will be with your friends. All the others are going. Anyway it won't be for long.' . . . 'I don't care about the others. I am not a parcel. I am not going with them.'

> My aunt, with an insight, that was not altogether typical of her, gave in, and we trotted home to her little house in Bow where my uncle greeted us with surprise. A few days later my aunt and uncle evacuated themselves with me and I was spared the trauma of a second separation.[3]

Martha and her foster mother ended up living in Devon, with her foster father only joining them at weekends, while working as a black cab driver in London during the week. Many other Kindertransport refugees were evacuated with their schools and without their foster families. Some later recounted that the rural families who were supposed to take them in showed reluctance to accommodate them because of their German accents or because they were Jewish.

Many British people clearly had an inadequate understanding of the political situation on the Continent in general, and the situation of those who had fled to the UK in particular. A number of Kindertransport refugees reported being discriminated against or being bullied because they were German or German-speaking – and thus, after the outbreak of hostilities, the enemy. Some British people did not understand the particular situation of refugees who had had to leave and find sanctuary in the UK because they were persecuted as Jews by the Nazi government.

Kindertransport refugee Anita Alpern (later Anita Jaye), who, like Martha Blend, was also based in rural Devon, recalled that there were local people who 'didn't know what Jews were. They wouldn't have been a bit surprised if we did have the horns. They didn't understand the concept of being Jewish at all.'[4] Likewise, Dora Sklut described a similar experience when she was evacuated to the countryside and placed with a Christian family:

Now, they had never seen Jewish people before. They were nice people in their own way, but they didn't know any better. And the husband wanted to know what a Jew, what it was like. They really believed – this is not a joke – he thought Jews had horns. I couldn't understand. I said, 'Do I look like I have horns?' I thought he was joking. No, he actually believed that.[5]

Not only school children experienced evacuation: Bea Green was evacuated while a student in the Education Department at University College London. The whole department was evacuated to Aberystwyth. She generally enjoyed her time in Wales, but experienced some anti-Semitism from a fellow student, though not out of ignorance but out of ideological conviction. This fellow student called Stan Price had been a Nazi sympathizer when he was a younger man:

> He took up again his original ideas of, you know, of the Herrenvolk and superior . . ., racial superiority and all of that and spouted this publicly. When he realized that it upset me . . . he said 'Well, you know, you're all right.' You know, the argument you're all right, it's all the other Jews. And I remember there – because of the way he spoke – one couldn't actually argue against him, because there was nothing tangible to argue; it was an attitude which was so entrenched and so profoundly ill thought out, that certainly at that stage there was nothing, I felt there was nothing I could do about Stan Price. So, I remember I walked down to the beach . . . and I sat on the pebbles and wept into the sea. I was just so frustrated and so upset thinking that here I'd come away from this thing only to meet it again.[6]

Possible public resentment against German-speaking individuals was openly discussed in refugee groups at the time. Kindertransport refugee Benno Black, who arrived in June 1939, recalled how the man from the Jewish Refugee Committee 'called us all into the office . . . he said, "Don't speak German on the street in public", because he's heard complaints about it. "People don't like it, because we're at war with Germany. So don't speak German."'[7]

Many children were forced or encouraged to change their name to something less German or less foreign-sounding. While this effort may appear on its face to be practical, it made many feel that there was an attempt to remove or dismiss the culture and ethnic persona of the child. Benno, after spending the first nine months in a communal setting, was sent with two other boys to live with an elderly couple in Northampton, where the landlady told them, '"That sounds too German. I'm going to give you three boys English names."' He continues: 'So my name was Reginald or Reg for short. And the other boy's name was Günther. He became John. And the other boy's name was Karl, and he became Peter.'[8]

Martha Blend recalled how her classmates decided she was a German spy after hearing her surname, Immerdauer. They made her life 'as uncomfortable as possible' and used to chase her, try to trip her up and punch her after school.[9]

It was not only children who engaged in discrimination and bullying: Kurt Treitel remembered how those in the positions of power actively discriminated against those they perceived as different. In May 1940, Kurt Treitel's 11-year-old brother Günther was expelled from school for being German:

> [W]e got a letter from this headmaster saying that in view of the events which have occurred on the continent, he did not feel that he could any longer harbour a German boy in his house. So there was this strange situation that at one time we weren't wanted because we were Jews; now he wasn't wanted because he was German.[10]

This feeling of experiencing again what one was trying to escape from in the first place unfortunately caught up with many of the older teenage Kindertransport refugees when it came to the matter of war-time internment. The UK government's 'Collar the Lot' mantra did not stop at Kindertransport refugees who were over the age of 16. It seems bizarre that the UK government first created a scheme to help them escape persecution and incarceration, only to incarcerate them during the war years in the UK, or even deport them abroad.

The Aliens Department of the Home Office had started to set up internment tribunals immediately after the start of hostilities in September 1939. The aim was to categorize all enemy aliens into three categories: those in category A were to be interned immediately; those in category B were not to be interned but might receive restrictions to their freedom of travel and where they could reside; those allocated category C were considered to be of no danger to the UK and were exempt from both internment and restrictions. There were 120 tribunals set up all over the UK, and by February 1940 they had finished categorizing all enemy aliens over the age of 16, both male and female. Among those given category B status were a number of teenagers who had escaped on a Kindertransport.

Those classified as category A were interned in camps being set up across the UK, the largest of which were on the Isle of Man. Others were set up in and around Glasgow, Liverpool, Manchester, Bury, Huyton, Sutton Coldfield, London, Kempton Park, Lingfield, Seaton and Paignton. Initially, all the other 'enemy aliens' who had been assessed continued with their lives, some with restrictions.

However, in May 1940, as the German forces advanced across Europe, and with the risk of German invasion considered high, a further 8,000 German and Austrian residents found themselves interned. The government was fully aware that amongst those that were now being interned would be many who were refugees from National Socialism. As Prime Minister Winston Churchill stated in the House of Commons on 4 June 1940:

> We have found it necessary to take measures of increasing stringency, not only against enemy aliens and suspicious characters of other nationalities, but also against British subjects who may become a danger or a nuisance should the war be transported to the United Kingdom. I know there are a great

many people affected by the orders which we have made who are the passionate enemies of Nazi Germany. I am very sorry for them, but we cannot, at the present time and under the present stress, draw all the distinctions which we should like to do.[11]

Training camps such as the one at Gwrych Castle accommodated older Kindertransport refugees, many of whom were now affected by the government internment policy. The Castle's residents over the age of 16, regardless of whether they were male or female, child refugees or refugee members of staff, had to travel to Caernarfon and appear in front of the local tribunal when asked to do so during the first few months of the Second World War. Most were put in category C, but a sizeable number, even though they were known and recognized as refugees from National Socialism, were placed in category B. While most of the category B restrictions that were placed on the Gwrych residents in late 1939 and early 1940 were not too severe, the situation changed as the war developed. There had been a media panic about Nazis infiltrating British life and the possibility of German agents living in the UK waiting to support a German invasion from within the country. As early as January 1940, for example, the *Liverpool Daily Post* had speculated that 'Fifth Columnists' were active in north Wales.

Six months later, on 21 June 1940, the Chief Constable of Colwyn Bay, accompanied by several policemen, arrived at Gwrych Castle and took away a number of residents. They were marched through Abergele and then transported to Liverpool. This was repeated several times until 26 June 1941. Some of those interned ended up in the Hutchinson Camp on the Isle of Man, while some 'volunteered' to be transported abroad. The last residents taken away for internment from Gwrych were extremely unlucky, as the British government was in the process of revoking the policy of universal internment by June 1941.

Julius Handler, one of the *Hachshara* adult staff and the brother of the *Hachshara* leader, Arieh Handler, described the awful experience of having to say goodbye to a group of the same youngsters whom they had managed to save from imprisonment in their native countries. The fear the refugees themselves must have felt is difficult to imagine as they were now being arrested and faced an unknown fate at the hand of the British authorities. It must have been extremely traumatic for many, especially those with direct experience of persecution. It was also detrimental to the sense of community and purpose of the Gwrych Castle *Hachshara*, and contributed to its closure.[12] Overall, it is estimated that around 1,000 young people who had escaped to the UK on the Kindertransport scheme were interned for varying lengths of time and at different locations.[13]

The increase in numbers of internees led to the various internment camps running out of capacity for new internees and the UK government decided to ship some internees overseas. Following offers from the Canadian and Australian governments, more than 7,500 internees were shipped overseas. There were Kindertransport refugees on several ships, including the *Ettrick* and the *Sobieski*, and also the *Dunera* in July 1940. Several *Hachshara* residents ended up on the HMT *Dunera* destined for Australia. This particular voyage subsequently became notorious for the terrible conditions on board. Many internees were mistreated by the British sailors on this particular voyage, their possessions were thrown overboard, and the sanitary conditions were appalling on the long journey. After the refugees' arrival in Australia, they were imprisoned in Hay Camp in New South Wales. The fate of many adult refugees on another ship, the *Arandora Star* bound for Canada, was even worse. In the early hours of 2 July 1940, the ship was torpedoed by a German submarine and sank en route across the Atlantic. Over half of those on board lost their lives. New research shows that there were no Kindertransport refugees on the *Arandora Star*, as had been erroneously believed.[14]

HMT *Dunera*
Chronicle / Alamy Stock Photo

One of the Kindertransport refugees who was sent to
Australia on the *Dunera* was Gerd Hermann Bernstein (later
Bern Brent) who had left Berlin on 14 December 1938 aged
15. Brent's mother was not Jewish, and he only became aware
of his father's Jewish heritage after the persecution started in
1933.[15] His parents realized that they had to find a way for Brent
to leave Germany, and, to prepare him, they decided he should
leave school and undertake technical training. He started an
apprenticeship as an instrument maker with a company making
microscopes in March 1938. However, after the November
Pogrom, it became clear that he had to leave Germany as soon
as possible. Brent was a member of the Berlin Quaker Youth
Group, which alerted the family to the possibility of escaping
via a Kindertransport. He would later recall: 'When I boarded
the London boat train in December 1938, my childhood came
to an end. Nearly sixteen, I was about to change country and

language.' As a confident teenager, Brent enjoyed his time in London initially, and it was fortunate that his mother also managed to escape to London just before the outbreak of war. But, as time went on, both his work and his accommodation in the Sutton Refugee Hostel proved rather dreary. After eighteen months in England and aged 17, Brent actually volunteered to be sent abroad after he had been interned, together with several other boys over the age of 16 from his hostel. He later remembered: 'Internment was to most people a calamity. To me … it was a welcome change from the dreary routine of rising at half past five, slipping into moist clothes, downing a coffee and, still half asleep, joining the crowds of workmen converging on the inner London suburbs … followed by nine-and-a-half hours of clock-watching.'[16] Consequently, he decided that getting farther away from Europe was a good idea, and he volunteered to be sent to Australia.

Partially in reaction to the sinking of the *Arandora Star*, public opinion turned against the government's internment policy. This led to more and more internees being released. By February 1941, more than 10,000 had been released again, and by summer 1942, only 5,000 were left in internment camps.

Some internees also joined the Forces after their release from internment. Wolfgang Billig (who changed his name to Walter Bingham shortly before the D-Day landing) was another one of the teenage refugees who had lived in the large community at Gwrych Castle. He was interned, and upon his release he joined the Army. Billig had learnt to drive in Germany before he left for the UK, and improved his skills driving a milk float in Abergele. He then became a driver in the Royal Army Service Corps. He became part of the British forces that supported the D-Day landing in Normandy. On 6 June 1944, he drove an amphibious vehicle ashore in Normandy.

Driver 13117760 Walter Bingham then volunteered to become an ambulance driver attached to 130 Field Ambulance. In this role, he was sent to the front line and saw a number of dangerous attacks. During the so-called Battle for Hill 122, which was fought between 3 and 5 July 1944, his ambulance was hit and the officer loading the ambulance was killed and the medic injured. Bingham got away uninjured, returned to base to get another ambulance and went back out under heavy fire to collect more wounded men. For this, he was awarded the Military Medal on 19 October 1944, including a citation from Field Marshal Bernard Montgomery and a letter from King George VI.[17]

Before September 1939, refugees had not been allowed to join the regular British Forces. A special unit was established, the Pioneer Corps, in which refugees could enlist. Most Kindertransport refugees would have been too young to join up in 1939, but in subsequent years many did. It is estimated that around 1,000 Kindertransport refugees joined the Pioneer Corps, and that 30 of them lost their lives in the hostilities.

Some of the young refugees were adamant that they wanted to join the 'real' British Army and fight the Nazi enemies directly, rather than the Pioneer Corps whose purpose was to support the regular British Forces. Harry Weinberger, who fled as a 15-year-old from Prague, was dismissive of this special non-combatant part of the British Forces. He was of the opinion that the Pioneer Corps was a 'ridiculous outfit'.[18] Harry's family was originally from Berlin, but his father had moved his business as well as his family to Czechoslovakia. As described in an earlier chapter, Harry then joined his younger sister on a Kindertransport train at the last minute, possibly without possessing the correct paperwork. As a number of relatives, including his grandparents, had already escaped to the UK, and established themselves, he had guardians and some financial help, although little emotional support, in the UK. He was sent to boarding school soon after his arrival. Subsequently, he started training as an engineer while also training as an artist, his real passion. Harry felt a strong urge to engage in actual combat against the Nazis, and tried to enlist several times. He

was repeatedly unsuccessful due to the fact he was underage
and, as he reported, because he was German. In late 1944,
he finally managed to join up. He was not entirely impressed
with the basic training they received. To Harry, it 'seemed
like a joke compared to the book that I'd read on the Prussian
Army'. However, he felt happy that he was accepted despite
his foreign accent and his Continental origin. He left with his
unit on a boat from Ireland for Italy. On the two-week journey,
he saw the Northern Lights, and endured a storm in the Bay
of Biscay, before the convoy reached Gibraltar and zigzagged
through the Mediterranean via Africa before finally reaching
Naples. Harry remembered that they were surprised that they
did not see action as they had expected: '[We] thought the war
would go on for a long time, and it seemed that the German
army had run out of fuel.' Harry then joined the Jewish Brigade
(the Palestine Regiment), where he met many men he admired:

> [They] were all A1 physically and there were among them
> people who had fought in Spain in the International Brigades.
> There were people who had had the most incredible adventures
> before they could leave Occupied Europe to go to Palestine and
> there were only a handful of people really who had joined up
> from England. And I wanted to be with them.[19]

He even met a neighbour whom he had known in Berlin in the
same unit. It is clear that his story is told from the viewpoint
of an adventurous young man who had set out to defeat the
long-hated Nazis, and that he had felt a sense of pride when
he finally achieved his aim of being a soldier. However, Harry
also had traumatic memories, especially when he encountered
objects left behind after the Nazis had carried out their murderous policies against the Jews: 'When I saw children's toys
– a mountain of toys – that had been left when children had
been killed and when I saw what had happened to the people I
identified with I felt I didn't particularly want to live in a world

where that was possible.' Harry eventually returned to the UK. He became an artist and lecturer in fine art in England.

The outbreak of the war made most Kindertransport refugees' experience in the UK even more challenging. They faced bullying and discrimination and suffered from the deprivation that the war placed on the civilian population. They worried about their families and friends they had left behind on the Continent, especially since direct communication with them became extremely difficult. On the other hand, the war provided some Kindertransport refugees with a sense of community and a sense of purpose that many British people would also later remember. They were energetic young people and many joined the Forces or the Auxiliary Services and carried out other useful work to help the war effort. Some were greatly influenced by wartime propaganda, and this could invoke a sense of divided loyalties, especially in the children from Germany and Austria. Some were very worried about the danger of an invasion by the German forces; fear of invasion could trigger extreme anxiety, especially for those who had strong memories of Nazi persecution. In some cases, the causes of anxiety were difficult to untangle: one Kindertransport refugee was so scared of the V2 rockets that began to fall near the end of the war that he and his sister had to move foster families because their placement was located too close to where the rockets could frequently be heard.

7

Death

Admission saved the children's lives. Exclusion sealed the fate
of many of their parents. Three-quarters of the unaccompanied
children in England by July 1939 had parents left behind in
Greater Germany, in most cases with no means of support.[1]

This statement by historian Louise London reflects the harsh
reality of the situation most Kindertransport refugees and
their families found themselves in. However, this conclusion is
also unduly teleological: it was the National Socialist genocidal
mass murder that killed the parents, not the UK government.
Nobody knew with any certainty in 1938/9 how the situation
in central Europe would develop. What was clear by that year,
however, was that children and adults who were defined as Jews
by the National Socialist Race Laws were suffering extensive
discrimination and violent persecution. The UK government
knew that there were many more persecuted people in central
Europe who were trying to flee than managed to find a place
of sanctuary. The UK government also knew that there were
many more applicants to the Kindertransport scheme than
managed to gain a place on a transport and eventually arrive
in the UK. Parents wrote pleading letters hoping to influence

the decision-making process of the organizing bodies in favour of their children. Parents would also put pressure on the child refugees who had arrived in the UK to get them to help the rest of the family find safety. For example, some children went from house to house in their new neighbourhoods speaking to people about the possibility of getting their parents a domestic permit. Correspondence shows that there were some family members who put a lot of pressure on their relatives, asking those who had managed to flee to the UK to find them guarantors: 'Now I have written enough about what you need to do in order for us to reach our goal. I know that you are doing your duty, I do understand that, but when I see that everyone is leaving, then I have no other choice to plead with you again and again.'[2] However, in most cases, the children had next to no chance of facilitating their parents' escape. Instead, many were destined to learn about the fate of their families over the coming years – often not until after 1945, or, in some cases, not until decades later. Some details are still being uncovered today.

Many Kindertransport refugees would later have to grapple with the knowledge that they had been lucky to be accepted on the scheme while their families remained unable to flee Nazi dictatorship and subsequent murder. For a long time, most Kindertransport refugees refused to call themselves Holocaust survivors. They felt that this term should be reserved for camp survivors. However, the Kindertransport experience is intrinsically linked with the experience of persecution and the Holocaust. Like many researchers, I feel I am not entitled to make any judgement about other people's experience of persecution, and I certainly have no wish to rank people according to a hierarchy of suffering. Kindertransport refugees were once called those 'to whom nothing happened at all'.[3] However, as this book has shown, this is not true. There is no Kindertransport experience that was not affected by the murderous policies of the National Socialists.

A number of child refugees were able to gain a place on the Kindertransport while their brothers and sisters had not. Ellen Davis, the Orthodox Jewish girl from the village of Hoof in the state of Hesse in Germany, was the only one of seven children in her family who was given a place on a Kindertransport, while her six siblings and her mother were murdered. This responsibility of being the only survivor weighed heavily on her. She remembered that photos were taken of all her siblings, besides the two very young ones, and that she was the only one whose application was successful. Otto Deutsch fled as a 10-year-old from Vienna in 1939. His father had been arrested and his mother was desperate to find a way to get him and his sister to safety. She put in applications for both Otto and his sister, but the sister was considered too old for the Kindertransport. Mother and sister were deported to Maly Trostenets concentration camp in Belarus where both were murdered.[4]

While letters were a welcome connection between Kindertransport refugees and families during the refugees' first months of their stay abroad, they would sometimes also be the bearer of terrible news. Martha Blend recalled receiving a letter when she was 10 years old telling her that her birth mother had been informed of the death of her birth father, but as her foster mother did not help her to process the news, she suppressed it and it only came back into consciousness five years later. In her memoir, she wrote about the complicated process of forgetting and remembering this traumatic news:

> In fact, I had 'forgotten' an incident that occurred five years earlier in the early spring of 1940 when I was ten years old and even continued to do so while writing this account. It now comes back to me in all its horror. I received an official looking letter from the Red Cross addressed to me. When I opened it, it said that my mother had been informed of the death of her

husband. My aunt found me sobbing hysterically, and unable to read the letter herself, demanded to know the cause of my outburst of grief. When I told her she insisted 'No, it's not true.' I knew this for a false and foolish reassurance, yet such is one's desire not to believe the worst, that I was half persuaded to believe her denial. To add to my confusion I received the last letter from my mother.[5]

While the situation of Martha's foster family was a very specific one, where her foster mother was illiterate and was not able to read the letter, this description shows several troubling aspects of the situation Kindertransport refugees found themselves in. It shows that neither the families nor the child refugees were given any support for dealing with this situation, nor any advice of what to do next after receiving such news about the death of a parent. Martha was so young and had no adult help on how to deal with this news or her grief; it is therefore not surprising that she slipped into a different reality and held on to the idea that her father might still be alive. However, by the end of the Second World War, and now aged 15, she was certain that her parents were not alive any more. She later described in her memoir how she did not actively think of her birth parents and their murder until many years later, to protect herself.

Less common was the news that a child who had been on a Kindertransport had died. Felix Plaut had fled on a Kindertransport aged 15, while his parents Alice and Emil Plaut remained in Frankfurt waiting for their visa for the USA to come through. It was their plan to then emigrate to the USA together. The Plauts were not the only parents of Kindertransport refugees who thought that their children would be safer in the UK while they were waiting for their visas to come through than they would have been in Germany. In a letter dated 10 December 1939, Emil told his son that their application to emigrate to the USA was making good progress and that their joint departure was therefore getting closer. He told Felix that he would need to help earn a living for the family in the USA and that he should try to learn a skill that would be useful. In particular, Emil advised him to improve his sewing skills. In the return letter dated 31 December 1939, Felix wrote that he was pleased that the joint emigration was imminent, and he also wrote about the everyday matters of a teenager, such as the fact that he was looking for a new stamp for his stamp collection. Felix ended the letter by writing that he was counting the days until the family were together again. However, Felix died of a cerebral haemorrhage on 21 January 1940. Letters of other relatives and friends show that there was a thorough investigation into the cause of his death, but outside influence and suicide could be ruled out. The RCM and his parents in Germany were informed. It was a tragedy in tragic circumstances.[6]

Some Kindertransport refugees became the only survivors of large extended families, changing their present and future lives forever. Even though many would go on to have their own families in time, what happened would influence generations to come. Their children would not have grandparents, and their extended family would be small. Some Kindertransport refugees married others who had had similar experiences. In an obituary for two former Kindertransport refugees, Marga and Frank Forester, their daughter Carole describes them as a 'tiny family' with no older relatives. As she notes, this might have affected her education and career choices as well: 'We were a tiny family of three, and it could not have been easy for them to encourage me to go to a college that was far away and to study abroad for a year, both of which I did.'[7] Marga was born Marga Levy in Germany, and Frank was born Franz Fernbach in 1925 in Gleiwitz, then Germany, now Gliwice in Poland. Frank arrived in England in December 1938 at the age of 13, and Marga arrived on one of the last transports, in July 1939, at the age of 15. The couple met in Birmingham,

Renate Collins in 2021
With permission from Amy Daniel

where they lived in the same boarding house. Frank served in the British Army and Marga worked as a cook for the British Fire Service, assisting the firefighters who were extinguishing fires resulting from German bombings. After first moving to London in 1950, Frank, Marga and their 10-year-old daughter, Carole, emigrated to the United States in 1956 and settled in Chicago. Carole remembered that her parents would always go out together. Marga and Frank died within a few months of each other shortly before their seventieth wedding anniversary.

Renate Collins found out after the end of the Second World War that all five relatives she could remember from her life with her birth family had been murdered. Being not quite 6 years old when she left Prague, she was only aware of her mother and father, her grandmother, an aunt and an uncle. This is not surprising as very small children only have a limited understanding of family connections. In time though, she found out from a second cousin, who also fled to the UK and lived in London, that sixty-four members of her family were killed in the Holocaust.

There have been some debates in Kindertransport research about the emphasis that was initially placed on the escape and rescue part of the operation, i.e. the part of the scheme that happened in the UK and would show the UK in a positive light. It has been argued that too little attention was paid to the fate of the birth parents and the birth families when discussing Kindertransport experiences. There is certainly some truth in this and the argument that the exclusion of the fate of the family left behind on the Continent made the Kindertransport look like a straightforwardly positive story: 'The *Kinder*, by the start of the twenty-first century, had become a safe story, put together neatly and with a redemptive ending.'[8] This way of representing the Kindertransport experience has been influenced by the fact that we do not know exactly how many of the Kindertransport refugees were reunited with one or both of their parents or other family members, or how many lost both parents, or, in some cases, all or almost all relatives, as was the case with Renate Collins. For years, many researchers, including myself, unthinkingly repeated that 90 per cent of Kindertransport refugees' parents were murdered in the Holocaust. This figure was so ubiquitous that it is difficult to see now where it was first used.

In 2007, the AJR, in collaboration with sister organizations in the USA and Israel, conducted a Kindertransport Survey entitled 'Making new lives in Britain'. The organization sent out questionnaires to over 1,500 addresses of Kindertransport refugees they had had some sort of contact with in the past. The survey also included a supplementary questionnaire which could be filled out by friends and relatives in order to give information on a Kindertransport refugee who was no longer alive. The response was good and 1,025 main questionnaires and 343 supplementary forms were returned.[9] The information that was provided by the returned questionnaires shows that 54 per cent of parents of Kindertransport refugees were believed to have been killed, and that 41 per cent of Kindertransport refugees never saw both their parents again. However, these percentages of surviving parents are contradicted by the findings regarding small sub-groups of Kindertransport refugees, such as the 150 children who fled from the border area between Germany and Poland after the Polenaktion. Of these children, 75 per cent were not reunited with their parents. These numbers have been used to criticize the validity of the AJR Kindertransport Survey's findings.[10] However, while being a valid piece of the larger picture, it is hardly surprising that these Polish parents had a much worse chance of survival than most others. They were trapped in a camp-like situation without a lot of chances for escape, and were already without papers, money or access to consulates and other agencies where visas could be obtained. In my opinion, there is no point in continuing arguments about these figures unless we can obtain reliable records for the majority of the Kindertransport refugees, which currently looks unlikely.

While a response rate of over 10 per cent is considered very high for a survey, there is no doubt that there is a self-selecting element to those who were able and willing to fill out such a questionnaire as the Kindertransport Survey. The AJR could only contact people who had made themselves known to a refugee organization. Those who did not want to engage with the topic, their past, or any form of organized group would not be known to the survey organizers. It is possible – and even likely – that former Kindertransport refugees who had the most traumatic experiences, which might include losing parents, would be less willing to talk about what they had undergone.

We therefore have to accept that Kindertransport research cannot rely on statistical data, and that we are unlikely ever to know how many Kindertransport refugees had to learn about the death of one or both of their parents, or of the death of their siblings or of other relatives and friends. With figures such as 6 million Holocaust victims (of whom 1.5 million are said to have been children), death was everywhere. And even those who were reunited with loved ones did not have an easy time.

8

Together/Apart

Regardless of the exact number of Kindertransport refugees who were eventually reunited with their parents, it is obvious that deciding to admit children only, without allowing the rest of the family to flee to the UK, was at the heart of the trauma most Kindertransport refugees experienced.

Almost all Kindertransport refugees had to part from their parents on the Continent, and arrived alone in the UK. It was extremely rare that child refugees did not have to spend any time without their parents. (Alf Dubs is the only child whom I recall who was sent alone on a Kindertransport by his mother only to be picked up in London by his father.) Some of the children were 'lucky', as one or both their parents managed to follow them to the UK quickly – in some cases, before the start of the Second World War. In other cases, children were sent to the UK on a Kindertransport to move them out of harm's way, and the parents intended to pick them up on their way to their destination of emigration. Siblings Stefan, Peter and Eva Kollisch had managed to get on a Kindertransport from Vienna and lived in the UK from July 1939 onwards, their father Otto managed to flee to the USA via the UK in August 1939, and mother Margarete Kollisch finally managed to flee

to the USA via the Netherlands in October 1939. The children
then followed their parents to the USA in April 1940. Looking
at the family's story with hindsight, the periods of separation
look short in comparison with those of many other separations
between parents and child refugees. However, the extensive
correspondence between Eva and her father shows how anxious she was about her mother left behind in Austria, especially
when war breaks out:

Dear Papa,

Today I write you a letter and I do not actually know why. But
I reckon I am surely not the only person who does something
on 2 September and does not know why, just to calm herself.
Please tell me Papa, is there really no possibility any more to
get Mutti out, really none? I decided to write this sentence
anyway, despite the fact that you will just laugh about it. Can
she get out somehow via Italy, there have to be trains running
on these routes.

Papschi, I have to ask you one thing: I know it is terribly difficult for you and us, but do not to get too anxious because we
need a healthy and for his years young father and Mutti needs
a healthy husband.

. . . So Papschi, keep your spirits up. Thousand kisses,

Eva[1]

Alf Dubs and his parents were reunited in the UK, after
his mother managed to get there just before September 1939
and the outbreak of war, and the five members of the Kollisch
family were reunited a few months later in the USA, their
mother travelling after the start of the war. But these cases
were rare, and, even if this happened, the children had experienced an initial trauma of separation because there was almost
always no certainty whether the parents would also be allowed

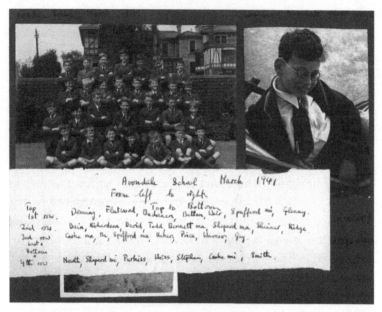

William Dieneman at his boarding school in 1941
With permission from Rachel Dieneman

into the UK, or whether the whole family would be able to flee together to a different safe country.

The general living circumstances of most refugees in the UK did not lend themselves to a stable family life. The Dienemann family never lived together permanently as a family again, despite both parents and both children managing to flee to England before September 1939. This was due to the impossibility of either achieving financial stability or finding suitable accommodation.

Not all Kindertransport refugees had entirely straightforward family lives even before their resettlement in the UK. Ruth Flatauer (later Ruth Parker) was born in 1928 and arrived in Britain in 1939 on a Kindertransport. Her parents were divorced, and, in Berlin, she was in the care of her loving grandparents and aunt. Her mother had mental health problems and was committed to a psychiatric hospital near Berlin. Her maternal aunt, Käte Jacoby, was one of the adult guardians for the individual transports. Käte was able to accompany several transports until she could no longer stay in Berlin. Fortunately, a few months later, she would manage to get a domestic permit for entry to the UK, and eventually Ruth was able to live with Lotte – her second maternal aunt – and Lotte's husband. Ruth has written her recollections of these years by telling of the different places she lived. Ruth was lucky in a way because she was able to live at least some of the time with her aunt Lotte and her husband, who loved her, and also with a number of English families. However, her mother was murdered by the Nazis under the T4 Euthanasia programme. Her grandmother died in the Jewish Hospital in Berlin, and her grandfather was murdered in Theresienstadt. Her family was fractured in more ways than one. In the UK, Ruth was happily married for sixty-four years to an Englishman who fought in the Second World War, and now has a large family.[2]

Some birth parents, and certainly some birth fathers, were not eager to be reunited with their children. Ellen Davis's father did not make any attempt to care for her after they both ended up living in the UK. After Ellen had left Germany on a Kindertransport and had been placed with a foster family, and her father had been freed from a camp and been transported to Kitchener Camp in the UK, he visited her once or twice but made no attempt to be a full-time parent. He then disappeared again by emigrating to the USA without taking Ellen.[3]

However, many others who survived were desperate to meet up again, even if the story of separation and reunion was not straightforward. Being reunited with their children was not easy, even in those cases where the parents managed to survive the Holocaust. Most birth parents and their children would have been separated for at least six years, and in many cases for much longer, as it was not easy to trace people immediately after the Second World War and it was also very difficult to travel. Children and parents had often changed independently of each other over this long period of time. Due to the circumstances of war and persecution, and the separation itself, both parties had been forced to cope with trauma and loss. On top of this, the children grew up and changed as one might expect from a young person growing up.

Ruth Michaelis (later Ruth Barnett) was only 4 years old when she left Berlin on a Kindertransport, together with her 7-year-old brother Martin.[4] Unusually, their mother seems to have been able to get the position of an accompanying guardian on their train and therefore was able to drop off Ruth and her brother before returning to Germany. Ruth's Jewish father had been a judge in Berlin before he had been forced to give up his job. He managed to escape to Shanghai, one of the few destinations in the world that was willing to admit Jewish refugees without a visa, an avenue that of course was open only to those who were able to afford a ticket there and were willing to take the risk of settlement in a very unfamiliar environment. Ruth's mother ran her own advertising agency. She was not Jewish, therefore not threatened by Nazi policies in the same way as her husband and her children. However, because she refused to divorce her Jewish husband, she also lost her business, their flat and most of the assets they possessed. She left Berlin and survived the war on a farm in southern Germany, near Lake Constance.

Ruth and Martin were able to stay together, which was lucky and possibly an exception. Many Kindertransport refugees were separated from their siblings and allocated different placements, sometimes hundreds of miles apart. Ruth remembered later how Martin would always explain to her what was going on, which she found comforting despite the fact that his explanation could not always have been accurate as he was still very young and only three years older than her.

Ruth and Martin lived in a succession of different placements, which was not unusual. Ruth experienced their first foster family as harsh and cold and was pleased when they were moved to the Quaker boarding school. From there, they were moved to the Godricke family who lived in Kent. However, their farmhouse was near an area where a lot of German V2 rockets could be heard, which disturbed Martin greatly. He was consequently moved to another family, the Haltings, where Ruth joined him after some months.

When the children were resettled with the Haltings, Ruth felt at home and she was keen to fit in and be treated like the birth children of the family. She decided to call her foster mother 'Mum', but her foster mother explained to her that she should not do this as she had a birth mother who would be upset if Ruth called someone else beside herself 'Mum'. Ruth remembered later that she argued with her foster mother and insisted that her birth mother was dead, as they had not heard from her. Ruth felt that her mother would have come to fetch her or join her if she was still alive. She found the thought that her mother was alive and had not managed to be with her – or the idea that she had not made sufficient effort to be with her – more difficult to cope with than thinking that her birth mother was dead. This is an understandable train of thought for a child who was 4 when she left Germany, and still only 10 when the Second World War ended. After the end of the war, the Haltings and the RCM made some efforts to trace Martin and Ruth's birth parents but to no avail. By spring 1949, Ruth and Martin had been living with the Haltings for four years, and the family were thinking of adopting Ruth, which would also give her the opportunity of becoming a British citizen. Suddenly, in May 1949, Ruth and Martin received a letter from their birth mother and, soon after, she visited with the intention to reclaim her birth children and take at least Ruth back with her to Germany. Martin was studying for his entrance to Cambridge University and therefore his birth parents did not want to make him leave England, but they did want 14-year-old Ruth to live with them in Germany.

It had taken the Michaelis parents some time to recover from the trauma of the war (Ruth in later life surmised that they had both suffered breakdowns after the end of the war), and it had taken Robert a long time to get back from Shanghai to Germany. He was keen to re-establish himself within the German legal system and took a job at the court in Mainz. Ruth's mother was still living in south Germany.

What ensued after the re-establishment of contact between children and their birth parents must have involved extreme emotional turmoil. Of course, the Michaelis parents wanted to be reunited with their children. Having suffered at the hands of the German Nazi government, they wanted to re-establish what they had lost and missed over the years. Having been unable to live together for years, they wanted to do so again, at least with their younger daughter. But for Ruth the very idea of moving to Germany and living with her birth parents was very far from a happy ending to her Kindertransport trauma. She had little recollection of her birth parents, she had little recollection of Germany (and had been taught that Germany was an enemy country and all Germans were the enemy). She did not speak any German and her mother did not speak any English. The parents remembered the 4-year old, but Ruth was now a teenager of 14.

Ruth's birth father started legal proceedings to have Ruth repatriated, and Ruth's foster mother, Mrs Halting, travelled with Ruth to Germany. Ruth remembered later that she did not have a passport but instead a travel document which stated that she was a 'PERSON OF NO NATIONALITY'. They travelled from London to Harwich to the Hook of Holland, which Ruth later described as a 'Kindertransport in reverse'. In Mainz, they met with Robert, Ruth's father, and Ruth's mother. Then Mrs Haltings returned to the UK. The Michaelis parents and Ruth travelled to the village of Unterreitnau in south Germany. Robert was able to converse with Ruth in English, which was useful, but he had to return to his job in Mainz, where he lived in a tiny room during the week, only joining his wife and daughter at the weekends. To say that mother and daughter did not get on, and that Ruth found it hard to settle into her new life, would be an understatement. Ruth was very upset and depressed, and spent a lot of time running out of the house and hiding somewhere or lying in bed pretending to be asleep. Ruth remembered that her parents talked about her in German every weekend, and the discussions often ended in a row. Eventually, it was decided that Ruth should go back to live with the Haltings in term-time and go to her old school. However, neither party had realized how difficult it would be to get a visa for Ruth to go back to England, as she was 'a person of no nationality'. Eventually this was accomplished, and Ruth, her birth parents and her foster parents managed to establish a successful routine of her living in England in term-time, and travelling to Germany in the school holidays. Ruth finished school, and later studied at Reading University. This case is one of the most extreme regarding adjustment difficulties in relation to Kindertransport refugees being reunited with their parents. The combination of Ruth being so young when she left her birth parents and the ten-year gap between leaving and being reunited obviously made this situation particularly difficult.

However, few Kindertransport refugees found re-establishing contact with their birth parents easy. Harry Weinberger was 15 years old when he said goodbye to his parents at Prague railway station and joined his younger sister on a Kindertransport.[5] Their grandparents lived in the UK and so did other relatives. Harry's parents survived the Holocaust and the war in Switzerland. Harry was sent to boarding school, studied engineering and also art, and eventually joined the British Army. As we saw earlier, he did not want to be part of the Pioneer Corps and managed to join a Jewish battalion of the regular British Army which was sent to Italy during the last months of the war. Harry had not seen his parents for six years

and, while in Italy, he got leave from the Army and permission
to travel to Switzerland to see his parents. Harry's experience
is not untypical of many reunions between young refugees and
their parents. He had last seen them when he was aged 15,
and he was now a man in his early twenties. He had not heard
from them or been able to communicate with them for six
years. Harry felt his parents were very different from how he
remembered them, and he felt that they were not interested
in him and what had happened to him. He felt that the meeting was 'embarrassing', and that they sat 'like strangers' at a
table in a restaurant at their first meeting. Such a description
makes the difficult expectations and the complex emotional
challenges clear. Harry felt that they never managed to have
a close parent–child relationship again. He also recalled later
that his younger sister received psychological therapy in later
life to cope with the consequences of the Kindertransport.[6]

Some older Kindertransport refugees started their own
relationships and family lives soon after their arrival in the
UK: Lore Heimann and Alfred Auerbach knew each other
from their sports club in their home town of Wuppertal in
western Germany. Alfred managed to get to the UK with the
help of a cousin who had married a British man. After his
arrival, he started working for the Oxford Refugee Committee.
When the Kindertransport scheme was announced, he was
asked whether he knew any children in Germany who needed
the Committee's help to come to the UK. In this way, Alfred
assisted a number of German children with their flight to the
UK and their placement via the Oxford committee. Sometime
after Lore's arrival in the UK, she and Alfred started a relationship. Extensive correspondence between the two after
the start of their relationship exists as they were separated for
long periods of time: Alfred joined the British Army, serving in
France in 1940 and then in France and Germany from 1944 to
January 1946. Lore lived with a foster family, the Buchans, but
was interned on the Isle of Man between May and December

1940. She was very unhappy about her internment and felt that her classification as a Category B Enemy Alien was unfair. She worried that the 'stigma may socially as well as economically gravely endanger our whole future in this country'.[7] Upon her release, she returned to live with the Buchans again, until she married Alfred in July 1942. She trained as a dressmaker at the Bromley School of Art before undertaking war work as a turner in an engineering firm in 1943.

Lore's mother Carla was Christian, but Lore's father Josef was Jewish, and on 30 October 1944 her mother sent a Red Cross message to Lore and Alfred stating 'Carla and Josef separated.'[8] Lore's mother was too careful to state this openly, but Lore knew that this meant that her father had been deported. Josef survived his incarceration in Theresienstadt. The parents were reunited with their daughter Lore, and son-in law Alfred and new grandchild, in 1947.

Kindertransport refugees were not only separated from family and friends. They were also separated from the culture and language of the country or place of their birth and, in many cases, from their religious background. Like Harry Weinberger, Vera Diamant (later Vera Gissing) also departed from Prague on a Kindertransport, together with her sister Eva, leaving her parents and friends behind. But, in contrast to Weinberger, Gissing had strong connections to Czechoslovakia, was keen on retaining her Czech language and was enrolled in the Czechoslovak State School. She emphasizes this in her memoirs by telling an episode about her father being spat at in his own home by a member of the German occupying forces for refusing to speak only German. She also recalled an incident in the UK when she met a fellow Czech refugee girl and was surprised that the other girl had lost her fluency in her first language and was only able to speak broken Czech.[9] 'Why is your Czech so bad?' Vera asked her, and the girl replied that she had been through a lot and had not had a chance to speak it. Vera vowed that this would not happen to her. She therefore decided to join the Czechoslovak boarding school despite having not only one, but two, loving foster mothers. This boarding school was a successful school which managed to instil a sense of national pride in its students, and obviously helped them to retain their connection to Czechoslovak culture and retain their language skills. Vera and the other Kindertransport refugees who had the opportunity to go to the 'exile' schools in the UK were in the rare position of being able to stay connected with the culture and language of their birth country. Most Kindertransport refugees were unable to do this. By the end of the war, some younger ones had little recollection of their birth country and its culture and language. Even older children lost language fluency if they were not able to practise their language skills.

Vera Gissing's mother was still alive when the British Army liberated Bergen-Belsen, but died of typhus soon after liberation; her father had been murdered earlier. Vera and Eva were repatriated much more quickly than many others: they arrived in Czechoslovakia on 27 August 1945. But, despite having kept up the linguistic and cultural connection with their birth country, they found their return to Czechoslovakia hard. Vera later remembered: 'There was no one to meet me, but then there was no one to meet any of us.'[10] They did not receive much help from the state despite being classified as 'war orphans'. Yet again, Vera joined a new school, and she was horrified that neither her fellow students nor the teachers were friendly to her. She was eyed with suspicion and the others believed that she had spent the war years in the relative safety of the UK while the Czechs who had remained in the country had had to suffer the Nazi occupation. But Vera felt that the anti-Semitic propaganda of the Nazi occupiers had also had a negative influence on her fellow classmates, so that they were not therefore sympathetic towards the returning Jewish children. While she did manage to meet some of her old friends who had not forgotten her, and was even reunited with her pet cat, she also experienced many disappointments in trying to recover her former life. Despite feeling discriminated against at school, she finished her exams and enrolled at the university in Prague in 1947. However, things did not improve at university: her boyfriend was given the nickname 'Jew lover' by the other students. Furthermore, the political situation in Czechoslovakia was changing in a direction that Vera was not happy with and so she decided to return to the UK. Accordingly, the last chapter of her memoir is entitled 'British by choice'.

An important criticism of the Kindertransport scheme concerns its apparent lack of effort to enable the children to grow up within their own religious community. As discussed earlier in this book, there were not enough Jewish foster placements or sufficient opportunity to join a Jewish-led communal setting to make it easy for the Kindertransport refugees to grow up in an environment that would reflect their birth families. The RCM had been extremely slow to set up structures to support the child refugees' religious education while they were placed in non-Jewish settings, and were generally slow even to acknowledge this issue, which would become a subject for fierce debate during the later years of the Second World War.

The lack of opportunity for Jewish religious instruction or Jewish community was often brought to the attention of the RCM by the child refugees themselves, depending on the age and character of the child, or by relatives who were in contact with the child and wrote to the RCM. The organization would then investigate the matter and generally remove the child from the placement if the child was very unhappy and a new placement could be found. If the child was happy, the RCM tended to overlook the problem of religious adherence and leave the child in their placement. As discussed before, the procedures of the regional and sub-committees of the RCM were not consistent.

Rabbi Solomon Schonfeld and other representatives of the Orthodox communities, such as Harry Goodman, openly criticized the RCM repeatedly, and their campaign culminated in the publication of a pamphlet entitled 'The child estranging movement: an exposé on the alienation of Jewish refugee children in Great Britain from Judaism' in 1944.[11] At the time, a number of complex positions and forces were at play. The RCM saw itself as non-denominational and, as we can see from their annual reports during wartime, they were committed to presenting the Kindertransport scheme as a success. This can be seen from the grateful letters from child refugees they include in their report, as well as lists of Kindertransport refugees who were high achievers in education and training. The RCM also favoured children's placements in foster families, rather than communal settings. Naturally, Rabbi Schonfeld and his allies saw the children's adherence to Judaism, and particularly Orthodox Judaism, as an overriding aim for their care. Schonfeld and his allies therefore preferred the children to be placed in communal homes, as there were clearly not enough Orthodox foster families. There was no Orthodox involvement in the leadership of the RCM: the leadership was non-Jewish, and its Jewish welfare officer was not from the Orthodox community but a member of the liberal Reform community.

One of the most high-profile cases discussed at the time was the situation of six Polish Jewish Kindertransport refugees who were evacuated from London to Talaton, a village in Devon. All were billeted with Christian families, and it was the relatives of Josef Kamiel who contacted the RCM from America complaining that the boy was 'out of touch with members of his own faith' despite the explicit instructions of his birth parents. When the RCM investigated this accusation in 1940, it received an angry response from the foster carers of Josef and two other boys, stating that he was receiving daily Hebrew instruction from a teacher who had accompanied the children from London, and that they enabled him to observe the Sabbath.[12] Josef remained with his foster carer while the two other boys left Devon to join relatives abroad. Then, the teacher who had given the Hebrew lessons, along with many other evacuees, left to return to London but Josef still remained, as did three Polish Jewish refugee girls who had been part of the same evacuation and had also been billeted with a Christian family. The RCM tolerated this for a considerable length of time but then decided that the children were now around 14 years old and needed to be moved to a Jewish placement. As such a length of time had now elapsed, this caused Josef tremendous stress as he now did not wish to move. In a report, it was stated that he had started wetting the bed and was very unsettled. A gradual acclimatization to a new Jewish environment was suggested, and it was noted that Josef's current foster parents would not oppose such a move. In the end, Josef was not moved, and neither were the three girls. In 1946, the three girls were baptized. The news caused anger in certain parts of the Jewish community, and the Board of Deputies launched an enquiry. The resulting report blamed the authorities and the UK government for not giving any thought to the aftercare of the Kindertransport refugees beyond the initial arrival period. This valid criticism is borne out by several issues discussed here and in the following chapter.

Clearly, forcible estrangement of a child from their religious and cultural background is a serious matter. This process had consequences for many who would later feel that they could not live within a Jewish community even if they wished to, or that they would be forever estranged from their birth family even if they survived. There are also some extreme cases of even more forcible estrangement of child refugees from their background, which can only be described as criminal and child abuse. As late as 2017, new stories emerged of former Kindertransport refugees who were not brought up as their birth parents had wished and whose foster parents' denial of their religious roots led to a tragic outcome. Fred and Gerda Taylor were placed with a Christadelphian couple after their arrival in the UK on a Kindertransport, despite their birth mother's explicit instruction that they should be raised within the Jewish faith. Fred recalled being abused emotionally and physically by his foster parents who – not unlike Susi Bechhöfer's foster parents – wanted to have complete control over the children. This went as far as lying to the children's birth family when the birth family tried to get in touch with the children. Fred and Gerda's whole family had in fact managed to emigrate to Palestine and made several attempts to contact the children in the 1940s and 1950s. The Christadelphian foster parents lied to the children's birth mother, saying that the children did not want any contact with her. They even misled the police. When the police were instructed to check on the children, the foster parents lied and said they did not know anything about their whereabouts – while in fact they were still living with the family. Fred recalled how heartbroken he was when he found this out and realized that his mother must have believed for the rest of her life that he did not want to have contact with her – which was very far from the truth.[13]

9

Life

Life in the immediate post-war years was tough for many people, but especially for the Kindertransport refugees in the UK. Some of the younger children were still underage and stayed with their foster parents. Some of the foster parents, upon learning of the birth parents' deaths, adopted the child. This was the case with Renate Collins, for example, who was adopted by her foster parents in 1947. However, once the children became adults, they were faced with the decision of where to go and what to do. Naturalization was an issue which was discussed within refugee circles and in the UK Parliament from the early 1940s onwards. The wartime Home Secretary Herbert Morrison argued repeatedly against giving assurances to refugees that they would be naturalized automatically after the war. For example, on 14 October 1943, Eleanor Rathbone MP, a tireless campaigner on refugee issues, asked Morrison in the House of Commons whether assurance could at least be given to those refugees who were fighting in the Forces. Morrison refused:

> Miss Rathbone: Could not some assurance be given to aliens who are serving in the Armed Forces and yet are quite uncertain

as to whether, after the war is over, they will not be bundled out of this country? If they are good enough to serve in the British or Allied Forces, are they not good enough for naturalisation?

Mr. Morrison: I would not accept that. I think it would be most unwise that such a sweeping commitment should be entered into. The question of naturalisation must be kept open to be settled on its merits in due course.[1]

Clearly, this policy did not contribute to the refugees' feeling of security at the time. During the war, the temporariness of their stay was repeatedly discussed. The RCM Annual Reports emphasized again and again that the Kindertransport refugees were destined for further emigration once they were old enough and had been trained in the UK. The reports published case studies of young people who had successfully migrated onwards during the war. Some refugees were very worried that they might be repatriated after the war, which is understandable as they had no way of knowing what shape or form post-war Europe would take. A publication by the Association of Jewish Refugees noted: 'This feeling of insecurity did not stop until the first naturalisations actually took place.'[2]

In the end, after the Second World War, many of the refugees from National Socialism who were over 18 years old and wished to remain in the UK did become naturalized. The process of applying to become a UK citizen was relatively straightforward, and many of the then adult Kindertransport refugees successfully applied. However, not all saw the fee of £10 that had to be paid as fair, especially those who had fought in the British Forces in the war.

The Kindertransport refugees now had to establish a life for themselves, coping with the trauma of what happened to them, and in many cases with very little support from family, friends or any other agencies. Some were disappointed by the educational opportunities that were offered to them. Some found it difficult to obtain a job in a post-war Britain that was suffering a multitude of challenges. This led to many Kindertransport refugees moving to more prosperous or economically active areas within the UK, or even leaving the UK and moving abroad, for example to the USA, which looked like the land of opportunity to many of the young people. Some also moved to join family members who had managed to establish a new life in other countries.

I have previously discussed our inability to provide precise statistical information regarding the further lives of the Kindertransport refugees, but from the life histories researched it is almost certain that the majority stayed in the UK. It is also clear that only a very small number of the Kindertransport refugees wished to return to the countries of their birth; to Germany, Austria, Czechoslovakia or Poland. Those refugees whose parents were still alive and where the parents decided to live in their originating country might have been persuaded, but this seems to have been the case with very few Kindertransport refugees. The previous chapter discusses how Ruth Barnett was repatriated against her will and how, when this did not work out, she returned to be educated in the UK, where she has lived ever since.

Inge Backwitz (later Inge Lammel) was one of the few Kindertransport refugees who returned to Germany, despite the fact that her parents had been murdered and that she had very few relatives there.[3] In her case, it was a political decision: she wanted to help build the new socialist, anti-fascist German Democratic Republic. Lammel was born on 8 May 1924 in the Prenzlauer Berg district of Berlin. Her father, Julius Rackwitz, was a bank clerk and the head of the choir at her local synagogue; her mother worked in fashion design. Lammel later remembered getting beaten up several times on her way to school after January 1933. Her father lost his job with Deutsche Bank in 1933, and later, during the November 1938 Pogrom, he was arrested and taken to Sachsenhausen concentration camp.

Inge and her sister Eva fled on a Kindertransport to the UK in July 1939. The suitcase Inge took with her is now in the Jewish Museum in Berlin. She was placed with two women teachers in Sheffield who helped the 15-year-old integrate into her new school and unfamiliar surroundings. However, once she turned 16, she was asked to appear at an internment tribunal and then interned on the Isle of Man. Fortunately, she was allowed to leave after six weeks and started training as a nursery nurse in Bristol. In 1944, Lammel moved to London where she met with other German-speaking refugees. She joined left-wing refugee organizations such as the Free German League of Culture, the Movement for a Free Germany, and the Free German Youth, all of which were known for their socialist and communist leanings.

Lammel attended the Victory celebrations in Trafalgar Square on her twenty-first birthday, but soon found out that both her parents had been murdered in Auschwitz. She joined the German Communist Party while still in London in 1946, and then left for Germany in autumn 1947 and settled in East Berlin. Her political convictions brought her to the Socialist Unity Party, and she remained a member of this party and its successor parties, such as the PDS (Party of Democratic Socialism) and Die Linke, until her death in 2015. She met her husband at a training school for party activists, and the couple had two children. She studied musicology at the Humboldt University in East Berlin, and wrote and published extensively on workers' songs. After German unification, she started to research the lives of Jewish families in East Berlin. In 2012, she was awarded the Order of Merit of the Federal Republic of Germany for her contribution to culture.

Inge Lammel's story is not typical of those that are often told in the UK to illustrate the history of the Kindertransport. She returned to Germany and had little further contact with the UK. Until about ten years ago, it was mainly the stories of those who became exceptionally prominent or otherwise successful

Retired nurse Lia Lesser in 2022
With permission from Morris Brodie

in the UK that were presented to the general public. But many others had more ordinary careers: Ruth Barnett became a teacher and then later a psychotherapist; Lia Lesser became a nurse; William Dieneman, a university librarian. The following three life histories might serve as examples of narratives of individuals who became very successful.

The artist Frank Auerbach is such an exceptional individual.[4] Auerbach was born in 1931 in Berlin and fled as an 8-year-old to the UK via the Kindertransport scheme. In his case, the parents knew the writer Iris Ogio in the UK and his sponsorship was a private arrangement. Auerbach became a student at Bunce Court School in Kent, which was an ideal place to develop his creative talent, and he excelled both in art and in drama. As a young man, he worked briefly as an actor, and he became a naturalized British citizen in 1947. Auerbach took painting classes at the Hampstead Garden Suburb Institute before enrolling at St Martin's School of Art, where he studied between 1948 and 1952. He also attended David Bomberg's revolutionary life-drawing evening classes at Borough Polytechnic.

In 1956, Auerbach was given his first solo exhibition at Helen Lessore's Beaux Arts Gallery, and in the same year his paintings were also exhibited at the Ben Uri Gallery, which to this day champions émigré and Jewish artists. He worked as an art teacher, first at secondary schools and then at tertiary level, before devoting all his energy to his paintings. He has had exhibitions at major galleries in the UK and Germany, and some of his paintings have sold for very high sums of money. The singer David Bowie owned an Auerbach painting entitled *Head of Gerda Boehm*. After Bowie's death in 2016, the painting was put up for auction, and it sold for £3.8 million in November of that year.

The life story of Lothar Baruch (later Leslie Baruch Brent) is that of an individual who clearly contributed significantly to ground-breaking scientific developments in the UK. Baruch Brent was one of the teenage Kindertransport refugees from an orphanage in Berlin who were put on the first transport out of the city on 1 December 1938, because it was feared that they might be attacked or arrested.[5] He was born in 1925 and lived with his parents and his sister in Köslin in Germany (now Koszalin, Poland). Because there were so few Jewish citizens in their home town, his parents sent him to live in the orphanage in Berlin-Pankow in 1936, assuming he would be less visible and safer there. This turned out not to be the case, and he fled to the UK in 1938. He was interviewed shortly after his arrival, while staying at the Dovercourt Camp. He later felt that he was chosen because he spoke some English. He gave a cheerful impression of the camp and said that they had had tea and that they had played football. Like Auerbach, Baruch Brent also became a pupil at Bunce Court School and was naturalized shortly after the end of the Second World War. His parents and his sister were deported to Riga and murdered.

After completing his schooling, he studied at the University of Birmingham and then completed a Ph.D. at the University of London. He became an eminent immunologist, and, together with Peter Medawar and Rupert Billingham, made discoveries about acquired immunological tolerance. They injected cells from donor mice into neonatal mice, which would as adults receive donor skin grafts without rejection. He was also active in Holocaust education and posthumously received an MBE in the 2020 New Year Honours list for services to Holocaust education.

Another former Kindertransport refugee who is recognized for her immense contribution to the UK is the entrepreneur and philanthropist Dame Steve Shirley.[6] Shirley was born as Vera Buchthal in Dortmund. Her father was Arnold Buchthal, a Jewish judge who lost his post due to the 'Aryanization' legislation that affected the civil service in Germany. Her mother was not Jewish, and originally from Vienna. In July 1939, Shirley arrived, aged 5, with her older sister Renate, as a Kindertransport child refugee in the UK. She was placed in the care of foster parents living in Sutton Coldfield. Shirley was later reunited with her biological parents, but also said that they never managed to re-establish a real parent–child bond again. Shirley later attributed her capacity to keep up with the constant changes in business and life to her ability to cope with the trauma she experienced as a young child.

Shirley attended the Oswestry Girls' High School. But as mathematics was not taught at the school, she received special permission to attend maths lessons at a local boys' school. She later remembered this time in Oswestry positively, as 'six wonderful years of peace'. After leaving school, Shirley kept up her interest in maths and worked in a technical environment. She became naturalized at 18 and took the name Stephanie Brook. She worked in the Post Office Research Station at Dollis Hill building computers from scratch and writing code in machine language. At the same time, she studied mathematics as a part-time student and received her BA. A number of appointments in computing followed and, after she married the physicist Derek Shirley, she founded a software company with the capital of £6. She later remembered that there was a lot of sexism in the workplace. She changed her first name from Stephanie to Steve in order to be taken seriously as an entrepreneur. She employed mainly female programmers, wanting to create jobs for women with dependants. Her company eventually employed 8,500 people and was valued at almost $3 billion. She also served as non-executive director for a number of high-profile organizations and companies, such as John Lewis.

Shirley retired in 1993 at the age of 60, and has since focused on her philanthropy. She is probably the former Kindertransport refugee who has received the most honours from the UK. She was appointed Officer of the Order of the British Empire (OBE) in the 1980 Birthday Honours for services to industry; she was made Dame Commander of the Order of the British Empire (DBE) in the 2000 New Year Honours for services to information technology; and, finally, she was made a Member of the Order of the Companions of Honour (CH) in the 2017 Birthday Honours for services to the IT industry and philanthropy. When asked about all her efforts in business and as a philanthropist, Shirley stated: 'I do it because of my personal history; I need to justify the fact that my life was saved.'[7]

These are just three examples of Kindertransport refugees who had very successful careers. But successful family lives also feature large in the celebratory narratives: the Kindertransport Survey showed that most of those who answered the questionnaire got married and had children. We have discussed the self-selective nature that could be influencing the results of this survey, and that those who see their lives as successful are more likely to participate in such a survey.

Additionally, as much as we enjoy stories that show us success despite adversity, we must also acknowledge the difficulties many Kindertransport refugees had to face, even after they entered adulthood. To mitigate against any false impressions, all I can do is provide examples of those who felt that they were negatively affected by their Kindertransport experience, and of the life histories of those who faced obvious challenges. In some life stories, we hear of very traumatic and painful events, which could have been mitigated with more support. Rather than just telling stories of escape and resettlement, and the establishment of a straightforward, successful family and professional life in the UK, we need to tell the stories of those whose life paths had more ups and downs.

Margot[8] is an example of a more complex family story: she was 14 years old when she fled on a Kindertransport. In Margot's case, her guarantors and her foster parents were one and the same: the family lived in London, but unfortunately the foster mother died and Margot had to leave the family.

Margot trained in tailoring and domestic science. She then went to work for an affluent household in England. While living and working there, she had a relationship with an American soldier who was stationed nearby. He was 28 and she was 19; eventually, she became pregnant. He had promised to take her back to the USA after the war and marry her, but instead he disappeared when he was posted elsewhere. It later turned out that he already had a wife in the USA.

Margot gave birth to a son in June 1945. On the birth certificate, the section for the name of the father was left blank. By the time her son's birth was registered, Margot had no job and very little support. Records show that the CBF, the organization that continued support for Kindertransport refugees after they turned 18, supported Margot between January 1945 and September 1949. They certainly checked up on her, monitored her progress and wrote letters on her behalf. Whether this was what Margot needed, we do not know. They also provided her with grants for a layette and loans for travel.[9]

After the birth of her son, Margot had to take many short-term jobs in different parts of England and Scotland in order to support herself. Unsurprisingly, life was very tough as a single mother with no relatives or support structure to help her. The CBF advised her to put her firstborn son in foster care, and in April 1947, an experienced foster carer wrote a letter to the organization and offered to foster him. Margot took her son to meet his new foster mother and left him with her. We can only imagine the emotional turmoil everyone was going through. Things remained difficult, and after a week the foster mother wrote again saying that she found caring for the toddler too difficult, even though she had fostered fourteen other children previously, and that she was ready to return him to his birth mother. This did not happen, but we know that Margot borrowed the train fare from the CBF in order to travel to where the foster family lived so that she could investigate the possibility of moving there and getting employment. This would have enabled her to visit her son. Unfortunately, this also did not work out.

Early in 1948, Margot took up a post in Scotland; then, on 24 December 1948, she wrote to the CBF saying she was taking up a post as a probationary nurse at a hospital in England. On 25 February 1949, the CBF notes that Margot 'was happy to have the child adopted'. On 19 September 1949, the last CBF entry says 'child has been adopted by his foster parents'. In fact, Margot's firstborn son was adopted in June 1949, and his name was changed. In 1949, Margot became pregnant again, and again she had to give birth without the support of the father. Margot's second son was born on in October 1949. He was taken for adoption just weeks later by a Scottish-American couple living in Glasgow. The records show that Margot had stipulated that the child be brought up within the Jewish faith, which was the case. Interestingly, she had made no such stipulation with her firstborn son, whose adoptive parents were notionally Anglican. From the CBF file, it is clear that the organization did not neglect trying to help Margot; there are many entries that show that letters were written on her behalf and enquiries were made as to how she was getting on. She was offered small loans and the RCM acted as an intermediary when an employer complained about her. Whether this was the support Margot needed is doubtful, and to this day there are different opinions among her children regarding whether the support of the CBF was adequate or not.

In the 1950s, Margot's life settled down. She married, the couple had three children together, and she worked in the family business and, after retirement, took on some voluntary roles. Margot's firstborn discovered the identity of his birth mother in 1979 after a thirteen-year search, and they met and stayed in touch until her death. He also established contact with his siblings and their families. Margot's second son did not find out about his birth mother until 2016, but he is now in touch with his half-siblings as well.

There were other Kindertransport refugees who had to give up a child for adoption because their family circumstances made looking after a baby too difficult. Gerda left on a Kindertransport from Vienna in 1939, aged 15. She found life in Britain hard and married very young. The marriage was unhappy, and when Gerda gave birth to a daughter in 1942, aged 18, it was already in the process of ending.

Later, Gerda recalled her situation and how, destitute, with little education and without the support of the father, she felt she had no choice but to give up her child: 'This, combined with wartime, left me no recourse but to have the baby adopted under the advice of the refugee committee.'[10] Gerda felt that, had she been in a better position, she would have kept her daughter, whom she named Sonya.

Sonya was adopted by a German couple who were living in the United Kingdom, but no further contact with Gerda was allowed. Gerda often wondered what had happened to her daughter, while Sonya wondered about her birth mother. Sonya's son eventually managed to make a connection with Gerda's step-grandson. Mother and daughter were reunited after 80 years in May 2022. Aged 98, Gerda lived in Canada, and her 80-year-old daughter travelled from the UK to see her.

Again, it is clear that too little thought had been given to the care of the young people once they reached 18, and especially after the war had ended. We cannot let the success of some overshadow the trauma of many. This should also influence how the Kindertransport is remembered today.

10

Memory

The Kindertransport story has impinged on the UK's public consciousness in different ways. One curious way this has happened is the popularity of the figure of Paddington Bear. Since the late Queen Elizabeth's Platinum Jubilee, there can be no doubt about the prominence of the stories featuring the lovable furry character in the UK. His creator, Michael Bond, confirmed that Paddington was modelled on a Kindertransport refugee: when Bond was interviewed in 2014 at the time of the release of the first feature film based on his Paddington children's book series, newspapers stated that Bond was 'inspired by memories of Jewish children arriving at Reading station just before the outbreak of the Second World War',[1] clearly referring to the Kindertransport. The Paddington books and films show an ultimately positive picture of British society's attitude to the newly arrived. Although initially met with suspicion, the loveable bear Paddington – originally from darkest Peru – overcomes these obstacles and integrates perfectly into British society, living with the nice middle-class Brown family.

Did this trajectory reflect the Kindertransport experience? I have shown with this critical history that this rose-tinted view of the scheme does not correspond to what really happened.

Lord Alf Dubs
Jenny Matthews / Alamy Stock Photo

However, the celebratory narrative remains prevalent: when refugees fleeing the war in Syria came to the attention of the British media and thus the wider British public, the Kindertransport was often invoked as a shining example of Britain's past humanitarian attitude towards refugees in the context of the present government's reluctance to admit refugees to Britain. The involvement of British politician Lord Alf Dubs, a Labour peer sitting in the House of Lords, in trying to persuade the British government to accept more refugees fleeing the Syrian war is another reason for this comparison between the two groups of refugees, even though nearly 80 years had elapsed since the arrival of the first Kindertransports in Britain. Alf Dubs tabled an amendment to the 2016 UK Immigration Bill asking for the government to admit more unaccompanied child refugees.[2] As discussed, Dubs fled to the UK aged 6 on a Kindertransport from Czechoslovakia, a biographical fact that he mentioned in his speech in the House of Lords on 21 March 2016:

> My Lords, ever since I tabled this amendment, I have been surprised at the level of interest, and above all support, from the wider public over the need to do something for unaccompanied child refugees in Europe. I declare an interest at the outset, as I arrived in this country in the summer of 1939 as an unaccompanied child refugee. This country at the time offered safety to some 10,000 children.[3]

Consequently, Dubs's identity as a former child refugee was mentioned in many media reports about the Bill and the Amendment. For example, on 26 April 2016, the *Guardian* published an article entitled 'Fresh proposal to help child refugees stranded in Europe tabled', which refers to the Kindertransport as a government-backed scheme:

> A new proposal to help child refugees stranded in Europe has been tabled and is expected to pass in the House of Lords on Tuesday evening, following the government's vote against accepting 3,000 children into the UK. . . . But, Lord Alf Dubs, the Labour peer who came to Britain as part of the government-backed Kindertransport scheme before the war, vowed to continue the fight and has tabled a proposal.[4]

In this book, I have shown that the government of the time initially only backed the Kindertransport in so far as it established the legal framework for this visa waiver scheme for children. It did not even consider committing financial resources or establishing a government agency to deal with the organization of the scheme – it relied on charitable donations, non-governmental organizations and a large number of volunteers. This had consequences for the scheme's organization, and for the experiences of the child refugees. Additionally, the decision that children only were allowed to enter the UK, and not their parents and families, caused immense trauma to many.

It is surprising that so many members of the public did not, and still do not, realize that the Kindertransport refugees were not orphans and that the scheme was not really backed by the government. How did these flawed celebratory stories manage to establish themselves in the public consciousness of the UK?

For many years, much of what was part of the public discussion of the Kindertransport was mediated through memorial efforts by the former child refugees themselves. The relative obscurity of the Kindertransport as a scheme, and of the fate of individual Kindertransport refugees, changed dramatically in the last two decades of the twentieth century. This was instigated by the former child refugees themselves who, from 1988 onwards, organized several large national reunion meetings and smaller regional gatherings. Subsequently, since the late 1980s, the Kindertransport refugees were also very active in writing and publishing memoirs and volunteering to give testimony in different ways. Understandably, many of those bearing witness to their experience were very grateful for being saved from being murdered in the Holocaust, and often expressed this gratitude by glossing over some of the more difficult aspects of their experience as child refugees. These memoirs were not written in isolation: authors heard testimony by others, and read texts written by their fellow refugees, and certain parameters were established which allowed for some narratives to be told and others forgotten. Many also felt that the negative experiences they had after escaping on a Kindertransport to the UK paled into insignificance compared to what those who had survived camps and ghettos had experienced. Over 1.5 million children are estimated to have been murdered in the Holocaust.[5] It is therefore understandable that former Kindertransport refugees still to this day feel that they were the lucky ones, and often do not define themselves as Holocaust survivors. But this is not to say that their lives did not include challenging – and, in some cases, harrowing – experiences, and that they were not affected by the Holocaust.

The parameters of what is told as part of testimony can shift over time, and in the case of the Kindertransport they definitely have. This happened because researchers have uncovered aspects of the Kindertransport that had not been mentioned in the memoirs or other testimonies. These aspects include the governmental decision-making processes, the selection made by the organizing bodies, the different types of placements that existed, and what happened to the former child refugees at the end of the war. In turn, the Kindertransport refugees began to talk about a more diverse range of experiences, including the more challenging and more traumatic aspects. They told more complex stories, which in turn started to appear in the media in the UK as well. During the eightieth commemoration, the *Guardian* newspaper ran a series of articles on Kindertransport refugees, and these included a portrayal of the challenges the refugees faced, such as unsuccessful placements, curtailment of educational ambitions and the complicated family dynamics between child refugees and survivor parents after the war. Other newspapers also published pieces featuring former child refugees who were more critical of the Kindertransport scheme.

Over the last thirty years, entrenched tensions between more 'traditional' historians, who wanted to rely exclusively on archival material, and oral historians, who felt that interviews with eyewitnesses and survivors were to be foregrounded, also affected the debate. To me, this is a false dichotomy. We will not be able to learn about precise organizational processes from the oral histories of former child refugees who might have been too young to understand at the time, and who might not fully remember by the time they tell their stories. In such cases, we need to look at the files of organizations. We need to match these with records of political debates in Parliament to unravel the complications of government intention and government policy. But to understand how these affected an individual, we also need to hear from them in their own voices – in diaries and letters written at the time, or through oral and video testimony or written text recorded in later life.

The historian Tony Kushner has argued that 'of all refugee movements in twentieth-century Britain . . . it is the arrival of what turned out to be close to ten thousand children in the last ten months of peace that has produced the largest number of histories, memoirs, exhibitions, plays, documentaries, films . . ., and memorials'.[6] We have many recorded voices of

Frank Meisler's *The Arrival*.
Kindertransport memorial,
London Liverpool Street
Network Rail

the Kindertransport refugees. We are less fortunate when it comes to the organizational records. There are two large gaps: the case files of the RCM are now kept by World Jewish Relief and are only accessible to the descendants of the individual refugee. The files of the German Department for Child Emigration, which processed the largest numbers of applicants, were destroyed in the hostilities of the Second World War. However, by investigating files from other organizations, we have been able to piece together general trends and policies. And by analysing life histories, we have been able to understand more about the challenges and trauma these trends and policies caused and how the Kindertransport and its consequences made those affected feel.

Why is there such a persistent desire to remember the Kindertransport as a largely positive story? Is it our understandable human desire to find stories of rescue among the catastrophic genocide that is the Holocaust? Or is there a desire of successive UK governments during the last decades to see the UK as more humanitarian and altruistic regarding its historical refugee policy than was the case?

In Britain today, the former Kindertransportees are a high-profile group who are celebrated and accepted by the British establishment. This manifested itself in honours for a number of Kindertransport refugees – for example, a knighthood for the chair of the AJR's Kindertransport Section, the late Sir Erich Reich. There have also been a number of receptions for Kindertransport refugees hosted by members of the Royal Family, and government ministers have participated in AJR events.[7] Both Lord Eric Pickles, who was appointed Special Envoy for Post-Holocaust Issues in September 2015, and the Secretary of State for Communities, the late James Brokenshire, spoke at the AJR's last major memorial event, 'Remembering & rethinking: the international forum of the Kindertransport at 80', in April 2019.[8]

As we have seen, prominent former Kindertransport refugees include the politician Lord Alf Dubs, the artist Frank Auerbach, the entrepreneur Dame Steve Shirley and the Nobel laureate Walter Kohn. Today's memorial efforts are largely organized under the auspices of the UK-based AJR in London, and also the North American Kindertransport Association (KTA). There are now also a number of groups where the Second and Third Generation (that is, the children and grandchildren of Kindertransport refugees) come together and organize events. Organizations such as the AJR have a legitimate interest in supporting their members. They need to seek funding and recognition from respective governments, and therefore they might also have veered towards an overly celebratory story of the Kindertransport, especially when their members also supported this way of interpreting the scheme. However, this has also changed over the last decade.

In the past, the Kindertransport has been remembered as a kind of British 'Sonderweg',[9] which is incorrect. There were other child rescue schemes to other European countries, and even to countries outside Europe. Around 500 children were sent to Sweden, around 1,000 unaccompanied minors were sent to the United States, and, as discussed, a sizeable number of those who fled to the UK were either sent farther afield or migrated farther. The memory of the

Kindertransport is therefore a transnational one, and other studies discuss this in detail.[10]

Some would argue that the persistent positive memory of the Kindertransport serves to detract from the UK's woeful record in shouldering the responsibility for providing sanctuary to refugees in the twenty-first century. Compared to other northern European countries, such as Germany and Sweden, the UK's willingness to admit refugees since the height of the Mediterranean refugee crisis in 2015 can only be described as inadequate. Compared to the large numbers of refugees that countries such as Turkey and other countries neighbouring Syria have admitted, the number of Syrian refugees in the UK is tiny. When the UK public demanded more action in aid of refugees from their government, the government initiated the so-called Community Sponsorship Scheme. This scheme paved the way for community groups in the UK to enable a family to come to their community if they could organize their accommodation, and show that there was capacity at local healthcare institutions and there were school places for the children. On top of this, the communities had to fundraise the sum of £4,500 per adult in the family to indemnify the government against any expense that might be incurred. Despite the differences – the scheme was for families not children only, and the families were entitled to state benefits and allowed to find employment – the similarities are striking. The UK government is again passing responsibilities to private citizens and voluntary organizations, rather than facing its responsibility. This is despite the fact that the UK is a signatory to the 1951 Refugee Convention.

The government's response to women and children seeking sanctuary after Russia attacked Ukraine in early 2022 was again similar: the 'Homes for Ukraine' was set up on 14 March 2022. UK residents could apply to host Ukrainian refugees in their own homes, providing they had a spare bedroom. Safeguarding concerns were immediately raised by experts, and the short-term nature of the scheme was criticized (hosts only have to commit themselves for six months and it is unclear where the refugees will be accommodated after that). A year later, most of the Ukranian refugees in the UK are still not able to return, and more long-term solutions have to be found.

However, despite the hostile environment different UK governments are trying to create, there was a sizeable proportion of UK citizens who were willing to help 85 years ago, and the same is true today. The public reacts especially strongly to the plight of child refugees. The news of the drowning of the 2-year-old Syrian child Alan Kurdi moved many, and led to the UK public demanding opportunities to help refugees. Even those UK newspapers that are traditionally hostile to a liberal refugee policy started to demand action to help children. This mirrors what happened in 1938.

Alf Dubs repeatedly referred to his own refugee experience when campaigning for a more humanitarian refugee policy in the twenty-first century. Of course, it is his story to tell and he is absolutely entitled to do this. However, Dubs's experience was not a typical one: when he said goodbye to his mother and travelled to the UK via the Kindertransport scheme, his father was waiting for him in London. When he uses a positive story of the Kindertransport to convince the politicians and public today to lobby for a more humane refugee policy, it is the real-politik decision of an experienced politician who knows how to play on the pride of the UK public and their sympathy for children. It does not mean that the Kindertransport 1938/9 is really something the UK can be proud of without qualification. (Alf Dubs and I met when we were both on a panel discussing the Kindertransport at the Imperial War Museum in London in 2018. I asked him why the emphasis of his campaign was only on unaccompanied children and not on whole families, even though all persecuted persons clearly had a right to sanctuary. He replied: 'Because it is easier.')[11]

The long life of the very charismatic and very humble Sir Nicholas Winton, who, without ever desiring it, came to personify the helper figure of the Kindertransport, also played a part in the positive memory of the scheme. Winton was 28 when he arrived in Prague on New Year's Day 1939, learnt about the desperate situations of the Jews trapped there, and then returned to London to organize the transport of Czechoslovak child refugees from the UK end. For years, his activities were not public knowledge, until they were revealed on a television show. Winton lived to the age of 106, which meant that for years he seemed the only person alive who had experience of the Kindertransport from the viewpoint of the organizer, during the time when public awareness of the scheme increased. He was honoured with a stamp by the Czech government; Prime Minister Theresa May mentioned him in her resignation speech;[12] and there was even a Google Doodle in his honour.[13] This meant though that, in many people's perception, the Kindertransport was the wonderful story of Nicholas Winton single-handedly rescuing child refugees and bringing them to the UK, where they lived happily ever after.

This book is trying to set the record straight and provide a critical history: the Kindertransport was a visa waiver scheme that helped around 10,000 persecuted children to flee to the UK. Most had to leave parents or other family members behind as these were not given permission to find refuge in the UK. The UK government neither financed nor organized the scheme at the time; it was financed and organized by a large number of volunteers and NGOs. There were many more applicants to the scheme than were successful, and many of the unsuccessful applicants were later murdered in the Holocaust. The hostile environment at the time meant that the selection processes that decided which applicant would gain a place were not always transparent and often not guided by humanitarian principles. The placements for the unaccompanied minors were not well prepared, and in many instances the children experienced additional trauma after their arrival in the UK. Internment and lack of support after they finished their schooling or left supportive settings left many feeling disadvantaged. The fact that many Kindertransport refugees managed to lead secure personal lives and have successful careers should not detract from those who did not, and from those whose mental and physical health were affected negatively.

Failing to acknowledge the real story of the Kindertransport not only is disrespectful to the memory of the Kindertransport refugees, it also does not help us make better decisions for the future. Rather than focusing only on the positive aspects of the Kindertransport and remembering it as a 'noble tradition', we should try to understand the reality of the scheme. We need to keep refugee families together; we need to prepare placements for refugees well; we need to respect their religious, linguistic and cultural background. Contact between refugees is important, as being able to talk about shared experiences is valuable. At the same time, it is essential for refugees to interact with a wide range of people in their new country. We need to enable young refugees to connect their past lives left behind in their originating countries with their new lives in the UK. As we move to an age in which there will hardly be any eyewitnesses left, we need to make an effort to understand the complexities of the past in order to work for a better future.

Notes

1 Myth

1 Jonathan Freedland, 'Pretending the Kindertransport was a part of a "noble tradition" is ignorant of history', *Jewish Chronicle*: www.thejc.com/lets-talk/all/pretending-the-kindertransport -was-a-part-of-a-noble-tradition-is-ignorant-of-history-2vi3ph YQmghjpshWnshPtH.

2 Christoph Gann, *'12 Jahre, Jude, 10.5.39, abgeemeldet nach England': Das Schicksal Eva Mosbachers und ihrer Eltern*, Landeszentrale für politische Bildung Thüringen, 2013, p. 38; also letter from Eva Mosbacher to her parents, 10 May 1939, original in German, Private Collection, Christoph Gann. All translations from the German in this book were carried out by the author.

3 Last message from Otto and Hedwig Mosbacher to Eva, dated 3 May 1942, reproduced in Gann, *'12 Jahre, Jude, 10.5.39'*, p. 67.

4 Barry Turner, *... And the Policeman Smiled: 10,000 Children Escape from Nazi Europe*, London: Bloomsbury, 1990.

5 Rebekka Göpfert, *Der jüdische Kindertransport von Deutschland nach England 1938/39*, Frankfurt am Main: Campus, 1999.

6 Claudia Curio, *Verfolgung, Flucht, Rettung. Die Kindertransporte 1938/39 nach Großbritannien*, Berlin: Metropol, 2006.

7 Louise London, *Whitehall and the Jews 1933–1948: British Immigration Policy and the Holocaust*, Cambridge University Press, 2000.

8 Jennifer Craig-Norton, *The Kindertransport: Contesting Memory*, Bloomington: Indiana University Press, 2019.

9 Vera K. Fast, *Children's Exodus: A History of the Kindertransport*, London: I. B. Tauris, 2011; Judith Tydor Baumel-Schwartz, *Never Look Back: The Jewish Refugee Children in Great Britain, 1938–1945*, West Lafayette: Purdue University Press, 2012.

2 Persecution

1 'Jewish population in Europe in 1933: population data by country', United States Holocaust Memorial Museum: https://encyclopedia.ushmm.org/content/en/article/jewish-population-of-europe-in-1933-population-data-by-country.

2 Marion Charles, *Ich war ein Glückskind. Mein Weg aus Nazideutschland mit dem Kindertransport*, trans. from the English by Anna Braun, Munich: cbj, 2013, p. 41.

3 Edith Milton, *The Tiger in the Attic: Memories of the Kindertransport and Growing Up English*, University of Chicago Press, 2005, p. 3.

4 Ruth David, *Child of Our Time: A Young Girl's Flight from the Holocaust*, London: I. B. Tauris, 2003, p. 16.

5 Oral history interview with Maria Beate Green, Reel 1, recorded 12 July 1996 © IWM 16784.

6 The story and the photograph of Michael Siegel were widely published in the North American press, and they are still easy to find on the Internet. However, various aspects of the incident were not reported correctly in some newspapers at the time, especially the German wording of the sign that Michael Siegel had to carry through the Munich streets on 10 March 1933. See 'The story of Dr Michael Siegel' by Eric Schmalz: https://newspapers.ushmm.org/blog/2017/12/19/dr-siegel.

7 E. Edinger, 'Ver Sacrum', *Blätter des Jüdischen Frauenbundes*, 1933, p. 1: Leo Baeck Institute Jerusalem.

8 In Ruth David, *Child of Our Time: A Young Girl's Flight from the Holocaust*, London: I. B. Tauris, 2003, Ruth tells the story of this friendship and its sudden end. She also recalls that the friend, Heinrich Hartmann, approached her when she visited the village forty years later. He had remembered her and her family and had kept a photograph of Ruth, Hannah and the youngest siblings all this time. Ruth took this as an indication that the initiative to end his friendship with her and the other siblings had been forced on him, maybe by his parents, and that he had remembered them fondly for over forty years.

9 David, *Child of Our Time*, p. 42.

10 Postcard from Alfred Dienemann (1888–1957) to his wife Erna (1899–1986), sent from Sachsenhausen concentration camp, original in German, Archive No. 2005/68/21, Jewish Museum Berlin.

3 Escape

1 Precise numbers are a matter of contention in this field of study as the UK government did not keep reliable records for statistical analysis. These figures are based on Louise London's analysis of government files, which is extensive: Louise London, *Whitehall and the Jews 1933–1948: British Immigration Policy and the Holocaust*, Cambridge University Press, 2000.

2 Transcript of the oral history interview with George Schoenmann, conducted by Mike Hawkins, Jewish History Association of South Wales, 20 September 2018, National Library of Wales.

3 See, for example, the autobiographical novel by Lore Segal, *Other People's Houses*, New York: The New Press, 2004.

4 See 'Love and politics in Llangollen: Fanny Höchstetter and Anton Hundsdorfer', in Andrea Hammel, *Finding Refuge: Stories of the Men, Women and Children Who Fled to Wales to Escape the Nazis*, Aberystwyth: Honno Press, 2022, pp. 101–11.

5 Quoted in London, *Whitehall and the Jews 1933–1948*, p. 99.

6 For aspects of the organization history of the Kindertransport, see Claudia Curio, *Verfolgung, Flucht, Rettung. Die Kindertransporte*

1938/39 nach Großbritannien, Berlin: Metropol, 2006; see also Vera K. Fast, *Children's Exodus: A History of the Kindertransport*, London: I. B. Tauris, 2011; see also Judith Tydor Baumel-Schwartz, *Never Look Back: The Jewish Refugee Children in Great Britain, 1938–1945*, West Lafayette: Purdue University Press, 2012.

7 Neville Chamberlain, *Hansard*, 'Refugees (government proposals)', HC, vol. 341, col. 1314, 21 November 1938.

8 Philip Noel-Baker, *Hansard*, 'Racial, religious and political minorities', HC, vol. 341, col. 1439, 21 November 1938.

9 William Butcher, *Hansard*, 'Racial, religious and political minorities', HC, vol. 341, col. 1452, 21 November 1938.

10 Sir Samuel Hoare, *Hansard*, 'Racial, religious and political minorities', HC, vol. 341, col. 1474, 21 November 1938.

11 Sir Samuel Hoare, *Hansard*, 'Racial, religious and political minorities', HC, vol. 341, col. 1474, 21 November 1938.

12 The Israelitische Kultusgemeinde Wien is the term for the formal Jewish Community in Vienna, which was in charge of the Kindertransport from Austria. The document referred to here is Completed Form 'O', dated 14 June 1939, original in German, Collection Israelitische Kultusgemeinde Wien, XXII. Fuersorge- und Wohlfahrtswesen, F. Jugendfuersorge, 7. Kinderauswanderung, Korrespondenzen ueber bereits abgereiste Kinder, 1938–1939, A/W 1962, Box 560, Central Archive for the History of the Jewish People, Jerusalem.

13 William Dieneman, 'From Berlin to Aberystwyth: the life history of a former Kindertransportee', interview with Andrea Hammel, 14 June 2011: https://pure.aber.ac.uk/portal/files/28123277/interview_with_william_dieneman.pdf.

14 Ruth L. David, '... *Im Dunkeln so wenig Licht'. Briefe meiner Eltern vor ihrer Deportation nach Auschwitz*, Wiesbaden: Thrun Verlag, 2008, p. 89.

15 Martha Blend, *A Child Alone*, London: Vallentine Mitchell, 1995, p. 32.

16 Milena Roth, *Lifesaving Letters: A Child's Flight from the Holocaust*, University of Washington Press, 2004, pp. 65–6.

17 See Ellen Davis, *Kerry's Children*, Bridgend: Seren, 2004. I also conducted an interview with Ellen Davis on 12 May 2012, Private Collection.

18 Davis, *Kerry's Children*, p. 46.

19 For a detailed analysis, especially of the Kindertransport refugees from Poland, see Jennifer Craig-Norton, *The Kindertransport: Contesting Memory*, Bloomington: Indiana University Press, 2019.

20 Stamp on back of child's identity document: Private Collection, Michael Couchman.

4 Organization

1 For the most detailed analysis of all organizations, see Claudia Curio, *Verfolgung, Flucht, Rettung. Die Kindertransporte 1938/39 nach Großbritannien*, Berlin: Metropol, 2006. For a detailed analysis of the Austrian organizers, see Paul Weindling, 'The Kindertransport from Vienna: the children who came and those left behind', *Jewish Historical Studies*, 2020, 51(1), pp. 16–32. For an analysis of the German organizations dealing with so-called 'non-Aryan' Christians, see Jana Leichsenring, *Die Katholische Kirche und 'ihre' Juden*, Berlin: Metropol, 2003.

2 See Ingrid Lomfors, *Förlorad barndom återvunnet liv: de Judiska flyktingbarnen från Nazityskland*, Akademisk avhandling, Historiska Institutionen, Göteborgs Universitet, 1996.

3 For a detailed discussion of the different Christian organizations on the Continent, with special emphasis on the Catholic ones, see Leichsenring, *Die Katholische Kirche*. The archives of the Bischöfliches Ordinariat Berlin contain archival material not found elsewhere. Unsurprisingly, the files of the Jewish organizations in Berlin were destroyed by the Nazis, whereas the files of this Catholic organization are much more complete.

4 Nicholas Winton kept a scrapbook which is in the possession of his daughter's estate. See also www.nicholaswinton.com/exhibition/kindertransport.

5 Merkblatt (Information Leaflet), original in German, I/1-96, Diozösearchiv Berlin.

6   Papers of Rabbi Solomon Schonfeld, AJ306/6, Parkes Library, University of Southampton.

7   Sir Samuel Hoare, *Hansard*, 'German refugee children', HC, vol. 345, cols. 787-8W787W, 17 March 1939.

8   See Susan Cohen, *Rescue the Perishing: Eleanor Rathbone and the Refugees*, London: Vallentine Mitchell, 2010.

9   For an excerpt from 'Lord Baldwin's Appeal for Refugees', a BBC radio broadcast aired 8 December 1938, see https://vimeo.com /117834111.

10   For more details on the Lord Baldwin Fund, see Richard Hawkins, 'The Lord Baldwin Fund for Refugees, 1938–39: a case study of third sector marketing in pre-World War II Britain', in Leighann C. Neilson (ed.), *Varieties, Alternatives, and Deviations in Marketing History: Proceedings of the 16th Biennial Conference on Historical Analysis and Research in Marketing (CHARM)*, Copenhagen: CHARM Association, 2013, pp. 82–105.

11   We have a nearly complete list of the 669 child refugees who escaped on a Kindertransport from Czechoslovakia, which includes information on guarantors and foster placements. See www.nicholaswinton.com/the-list.

12   Letter from Norman Bentwich to Dr Loewenherz, CBF, Reel 1, File 2.

13   For an extensive discussion, see Weindling, 'The Kindertransport from Vienna'.

14   IKG, A/W 1971.

15   Hahn-Warburg for the RCM to IKG, 27 February 1939, A/W 1971/2.

16   Exiner for the RCM to IKG, 10 March 1939, A/W 1971/2.

17   For Hans Lang, see IKG records, microfilm 0884.0126, as quoted in Weindling, 'The Kindertransport from Vienna', p. 29.

18   IKG to RCM, 11 July 1939, A/W 1971/1.

19   Aufstellungen über die Meldungen zu den Kindertransporten (List of applications for the Kindertransports), I/1-96, Diozösearchiv Berlin.

20　Letter from Dr Heinrich Spiero to Mr Roger Carter, dated 13 March 1939, I/1-96, Diozösearchiv Berlin.

21　Weindling, 'The Kindertransport from Vienna', pp. 20 and 29.

22　Interviews with Harry Weinberger, 12 January 1995 and 17 March 1995, British Library Sounds, National Life Story Collection: Artists' Lives: https://sounds.bl.uk/Oral-history/Art/021M-C04 66X0037XX-0500V0.

5　Placements

1　See Anita H. Grosz, Stephanie Homer and Andrea Hammel, 'Adverse Childhood Experiences (ACEs) and child refugees of the 1930s in the UK: history informing the future', 2020, pp. 7–13: https://issuu.com/acesupporthub/docs/aberystwyth_aces _and_child_refugees_report_eng__fi.

2　Letter to the Editor from Eva Hartree, *Cambridge Daily News*, 12 December 1938, p. 5.

3　Conversation between Ruth Schwiening and Ruth David, British Museum Sound & Moving Image Archive: Oral History Section, Reference #1500/1029 (8 May 2013).

4　Jeremy Josephs with Susi Bechhöfer, *Rosa's Child: One Woman's Search for Her Past*, London: I. B. Tauris, 1996; W. G. Sebald, Austerlitz, London: Hamish Hamilton, 2001.

5　Susi Bechhöfer, *Rosa*, Rugby: Christians Aware, 2017.

6　Letter, Lady Howard Stepney to Mrs Majer, 17 July 1939, Ilse Majer-Williams Collection, Wiener Holocaust Library.

7　Ann Chadwick, *The Little Girl Who Changed Our Lives*, Cambridge: Keystage Arts and Heritage Company, 2012, p. 28.

8　Refugee Children's Movement, *First Annual Report 1938/39*, Central British Fund, Wiener Holocaust Library, 153/11.

9　Central British Fund, Wiener Holocaust Library, 301/758.

10　Central British Fund, Wiener Holocaust Library, 301/759.

11　*Jewish Chronicle*, 23 December 1938.

12　Vera K. Fast, *Children's Exodus: A History of the Kindertransport*, London: I. B. Tauris, 2011, pp. 99–100.

13　For more information on the Kindertransport refugees at Gwrych

Castle, see Andrea Hammel, *Finding Refuge: Stories of the Men, Women and Children Who Fled to Wales to Escape the Nazis*, Aberystwyth: Honno Press, 2022.

14 Interview with Arieh Handler, Association of Jewish Refugees (AJR) Refugee Voices Testimony Archive (RV25). Arieh Handler was interviewed by Bea Lewkowicz on 9 July 2003.

15 Interview with Arieh Handler, AJR Refugee Voices Testimony Archive (RV25), 9 July 2003.

16 Hammel, *Finding Refuge*, p. 135.

17 Interview with Eli Fachler, AJR Refugee Voices Testimony Archive (RV103), 4 September 2005.

18 See, for example, Kindertransport ID Document, Documents. 9289, Imperial War Museum.

19 Sir Samuel Hoare, *Hansard*, 'Refugees (government proposals)', HC, vol. 341, cols. 1313–71313, 21 November 1938.

20 See Francis Williams, *The Forgotten Kindertransportees: The Scottish Experience*, London: Bloomsbury, 2014, especially pp. 56–80.

21 See Stephen Walton, 'Edith Jacobowitz and Millisle Refugee Farm': www.iwm.org.uk/history/edith-jacobowitz-and-millisle-refugee-farm; see also Gert Jacobowitz, 'Millisle Farm', *Belfast Jewish Record*, July 2006, 52nd Year (4), pp. 3–5: www.digital-library.qub.ac.uk.

6 War

1 Red Cross Letter, original in German, Private Collection, Renate Collins.

2 Red Cross Letter, original in German, Private Collection, Christoph Gann.

3 Martha Blend, *A Child Alone*, London: Vallentine Mitchell, 1995, p. 66.

4 Anita Jaye, interview 16323 Visual History Archive / USC Shoah Foundation (1996).

5 Interview with Dora Sklut, Kindertransport Association Oral History Project, 6 June 1998 (transcript p. 7).

6 Interview with B. M. Green, Imperial War Museum Sound Archive, Reference Catalogue #16784, Reel 6, recorded 7 December 1996.

7 Interview with Benno Black, Kindertransport Association Oral History Project, 9 June 1995 (transcript p. 5).

8 Interview with Benno Black, Kindertransport Association Oral History Project, 9 June 1995 (transcript p. 5).

9 Blend, *A Child Alone*, p. 72.

10 Interview with Kurt Treitel (Part 2), Kindertransport Association Oral History Project, 22 June 1999 (transcript p. 7).

11 Winston Churchill, *Hansard*, 'War situation', HC, vol. 361, col. 794, 4 June 1940.

12 See Andrew Hesketh, *Escape to Gwrych Castle: A Jewish Refugee Story*, Cardiff: Calon, 2023.

13 See Hesketh, *Escape to Gwrych Castle*, pp. 174–5.

14 See Rachel Pistol, 'Early internment camps in the United Kingdom: a forgotten heritage and history', in Gilly Carr and Rachel Pistol (eds.), *British Internment and the Internment of Britons: Second World War Camps, History and Heritage*, London: Bloomsbury Academic, 2023.

15 Alexandra Ludewig, 'The last of the Kindertransports: Britain to Australia, 1940', in Andrea Hammel and Bea Lewkowicz (eds.), *The Kindertransport to Britain 1938/39: New Perspectives*, Leiden: Brill, 2012. Ludewig's article and other stories of the Kindertransport mention that 1,000 Kindertransport refugees were interned (see, for example, www.holocaust.org.uk/kindertransport-overview) but I am unable to find a source for this number.

16 J. L. Brent (Brent/Berlin) in Berta Leverton and Shmuel Lowensohn, *I Came Alone: The Stories of the Kindertransports*, Market Harborough: The Book Guild, 2005, p. 48.

17 See Hesketh, *Escape to Gwrych Castle*.

18 Interview with Harry Weinberger, Sound Archive, British Library, 12 January and 17 March 1995: https://sounds.bl.uk/Oral-history/Art/021M-C0466X0037XX-0500V0.

19 Interview with Harry Weinberger, Sound Archive.

7 Death

1 Louise London, *Whitehall and the Jews 1933–1948: British Immigration Policy and the Holocaust*, Cambridge University Press, 2000, p. 118.

2 Letter dated 12 February 1939, original in German, AR 25058, Papers of Margarete Kollisch, Center for Jewish History, New York.

3 Doris Bader Whiteman, *The Uprooted: A Hitler Legacy*, New York: Plenum Press, 1993, p. 2.

4 Interview with Otto Deutsch, AJR Refugee Voices Testimony Archive (RV15), 8 May 2003.

5 Martha Blend, *A Child Alone*, London: Vallentine Mitchell, 1995, pp. 118–19.

6 AR25035, Felix Plaut Documents, Emil and Alice Plaut Collection, Center for Jewish History, New York.

7 'Frank and Marga Forester, Holocaust survivors', *Philadelphia Jewish Exponent*, 27 February 2014: www.jewishexponent.com/2014/02/27/frank-and-marga-forester-holocaust-survivors.

8 Tony Kushner, *Remembering Refugees: Then and Now*, Manchester University Press, 2006, p. 165.

9 See https://ajr.org.uk/kindertransport-survey.

10 Jennifer Craig-Norton makes this point in her book *The Kindertransport: Contested Memory*, Bloomington: Indiana University Press, 2019, p. 298.

8 Together/Apart

1 Letter marked Stockport 1939, original in German, AR 25058, Papers of Margarete Kollisch, Center for Jewish History, New York.

2 See Ruth Parker, 'Home from home', Private Collection.

3 See Ellen Davis, *Kerry's Children*, Bridgend: Seren, 2004.

4 See Ruth Barnett, *Person of No Nationality*, London: David Paul, 2010.

5 See interview with Harry Weinberger, Sound Archive, British Library, 12 January and 17 March 1995: https://

sounds.bl.uk/Oral-history/Art/021M-C0466X0037XX-0500V0.

6 Interview with Harry Weinberger, Sound Archive.

7 Letter from Lore Heimann to the Chairman of the Advisory Council on Aliens, dated 20 August 1940, The Gordon Family Papers, *Wiener Holocaust Library.*

8 Red Cross Message from Carla Heimann to Lore, dated 30 October 1944, The Gordon Family Papers, Wiener Holocaust Library

9 See Andrea Hammel, '"Why is your Czech so bad?": Czech child refugees, language and identity', in *Yearbook of the Research Centre for German and Austrian Exile Studies*, Leiden: Brill, 2009.

10 Vera Gissing, *Pearls of Childhood: A Unique Childhood Memoir of Life in Wartime Britain in the Shadow of the Holocaust*, London: Robson Books, 1994, p. 160.

11 For further discussion, see Vera K. Fast, *Children's Exodus: A History of the Kindertransport*, London: I. B. Tauris, 2011, especially 'The Orthodox experience', pp. 97ff.

12 For more details, see Jennifer Craig-Norton, *The Kindertransport: Contested Memory*, Bloomington: Indiana University Press, 2019, pp. 70ff.

13 Fred Taylor, 'My story', *AJR Journal*, 2017, 17(8), p. 4.

9 Life

1 Herbert Morrison, *Hansard*, 'Refugees (naturalisation)', HC, vol. 392, col. 1042, 14 October 1943.

2 AJR, *Britain's New Citizens: The Story of the Refugees from Germany and Austria*, quoted in Anthony Grenville, *Jewish Refugees from Germany and Austria in Britain 1933–1970: Their Image in AJR Information*, London: Vallentine Mitchell, 2010, pp. 53–4.

3 Günter Benser, 'Inge Lammel', in Dagmar Goldbeck and Anja Kruke (eds.), *Bewahren Verbreiten Aufklären. Archivare, Bibliothekare und Sammler der Quellen der deutschsprachigen Arbeiterbewegung*, 2017, supplement, pp. 62–71.

4 See Catherine Lampert, *Frank Auerbach: Speaking and Painting*

(London: Thames and Hudson, 2019); also Sarah MacDougall, '"Seen by the eye and felt by the heart": The émigrés as art teachers', in Monica Bohm-Duchen (ed.), *Insiders Outsiders: Refugees from Nazi Europe and Their Contribution to British Visual Culture* (London: Lund Humphries, 2019).

5 Baruch Brent, *Sunday's Child? A Memoir*, New Romney (UK): Bank House Books, 2009.

6 Dame Steve Shirley (with Richard Askwith), *Let It Go: My Extraordinary Story – from Refugee to Entrepreneur to Philanthropist*, London: Penguin, 2019.

7 Interview with Dame Stephanie Shirley, *Good Morning Sunday*, BBC Radio 2, 27 January 2013.

8 Margot is a pseudonym used to protect the identity of her family. Their names are known to the author.

9 Information and quotes are from a copy of thirteen pages of notes from the CBF, now World Jewish Relief, who supported the refugee pastorally and financially from 5 January 1945 until 19 September 1949: Private Collection, with permission from the oldest son.

10 Yvette Alt Miller, 'Holocaust survivor reunited with daughter after 80 years', 12 June 2022:https://aish.com/holocaust-survivor-reunited-with-daughter-after-80-years/?fbclid=IwAR0w7Vbn5I.

10 Memory

1 Julia Llewellyn Smith, 'Michael Bond: "I was worried that I'd let Paddington down . . .", *The Telegraph*, 23 November 2014: www.telegraph.co.uk/culture/film/11247595/Michael-Bond-I-was-worried-that-Id-let-Paddington-down....html.

2 The text of Amendment 116 A read 'The Secretary of State must, as soon as possible after the passing of this Act, make arrangements to relocate to the United Kingdom and support a specified number of unaccompanied refugee children from other countries in Europe': https://hansard.parliament.uk/Lords/2016-03-21/debates/AAE552DF-70A7-4220-8B67-D59EAA007FF4/ImmigrationBill.

3 See Hansard Online: https://hansard.parliament.uk/Lords/2016 -03-21/debates/AAE552DF-70A7-4220-8B67-D59EAA007FF4 /ImmigrationBill.

4 Karen McVeigh, Heather Stewart and Rowena Mason, 'Fresh proposal to help child refugees stranded in Europe tabled', *The Guardian*, 26 April 2016: www.theguardian.com/world/2016 /apr/26/fresh-proposal-to-help-child-refugees-stranded-in-eu rope-tabled.

5 See https://encyclopedia.ushmm.org/content/en/article/children- during-the-holocaust.

6 Tony Kushner, *Remembering Refugees: Then and Now*, Manchester University Press, 2006, p. 141.

7 See, for example, 'Charles marks Jewish Child rescue', BBC News Channel, Sunday 23 November 2008.

8 See https://ajr.org.uk/latest-news/remembering-rethinking-the -international-forum-on-the-kindertransport-at-80.

9 Literally 'special path', it refers to the theory that historic devel- opment in Germany was very different from that of the rest of Europe. See Jurgen Kocka, 'German history before Hitler: the debate about the German Sonderweg', *Journal of Contemporary History*, Jan. 1988, 23(1). In the twenty-first century, it is also used as a term to denote the divergence of a country's development.

10 See Amy Williams and William Niven, *National and Transnational Memories of the Kindertransport: Exhibitions, Memorials, and Commemoration*, Martlesham: Boydell and Brewer, 2023.

11 For a recording of this panel discussion, see www.iwm.org.uk /history/iwm-after-hours-new-perspectives-on-the-kindertrans port.

12 See www.independent.co.uk/news/uk/home-news/theresa-may -speech-child-refugees-nicholas-winton-syria-kindertransport -resigns-immigration-a8928771.html.

13 www.google.com/doodles/nicholas-wintons-111th-birthday.

Index

Illustrations are denoted by the use of
italic page numbers, and notes by 'n', e.g. 153 n.6